This practical resource gives inservice educators at all levels step-by-step guidelines and materials for bringing about successful curriculum change and development in any school or district.

Based on the author's 17 years of curriculum leadership on the local level combined with his experience as an adjunct professor of curriculum and administration, it provides a unique fusion of solid curriculum principles with proven techniques for putting them into practice in the actual school setting.

COVERS ALL MAJOR CURRICULUM AREAS

In a simple, direct manner, the **Handbook** first focuses on the importance of curriculum and curriculum leadership in today's schools, then breaks down the role of the curriculum leader by task, process, product, and decisions to show how he or she can be most effective.

Here's just an overview of the topics featured in each chapter:

The Significance of Curriculum Leadership
   Presents curriculum assumptions and definitions and describes how the position of curriculum leader has evolved to its current status

Curriculum Process
   Provides a specific and practical description of the day-to-day processes used in curriculum development, including a working model and procedures for conducting curriculum workshops

Curriculum Products
   Gives numerous examples of graded courses of study and curriculum course guides—the foundation for successful curriculum development

Curriculum Leadership Tasks
   Provides helpful hints on how to perform five different types of tasks efficiently, to allow more time for other curriculum leadership roles

(continued on back flap)

CURRICULUM LEADERSHIP AND DEVELOPMENT HANDBOOK

CURRICULUM LEADERSHIP AND DEVELOPMENT HANDBOOK

Leo H. Bradley, Ed.D.

PRENTICE-HALL, INC., Englewood Cliffs, New Jersey

LIBRARY OF CONGRESS CATOLOGING-IN-PUBLICATION DATA

Bradley, Leo H.
   Curriculum leadership and development handbook.

   Includes bibliographies and index.
   1. Curriculum planning.   32. Curriculum change.
I. title.
LB1570.B74   1985   375'.001   85-12164

ISBN 0-13-196056-3

PRENTICE-HALL INTERNATIONAL, INC., *London*
PRENTICE-HALL OF AUSTRALIA PTY. LTD., *Sydney*
PRENTICE-HALL CANADA, INC., *Toronto*
PRENTICE-HALL OF INDIA PRIVATE LTD., *New Delhi*
PRENTICE-HALL OF JAPAN, INC., *Tokyo*
PRENTICE-HALL OF SOUTHEAST ASIA PTE. LTD., *Singapore*
WHITEHALL BOOKS, LTD., *Wellington, New Zealand*
EDITORA PRENTICE-HALL DO BRASIL LTDA., *Rio de Janeiro*
PRENTICE-HALL HISPANOAMERICANA, S.A., *Mexico*

To Betsy, my wife, for twenty years of love and friendship. She is, incidentally, the best English teacher I have seen in a classroom.

And to my three sons, Lee, Michael, and Vincent, who are my hope, my pride, my eternity. They probably won't read this book, but the important thing is that they could.

About the Author

LEO H. BRADLEY holds an A.B. from Morehead State University, an M.Ed. from Xavier University, and an Ed.D. from the University of Cincinnati. He has spent twenty-two years in public education—five as a teacher and seventeen as an administrator. At the local level, Dr. Bradley has held the position of principal, curriculum director, assistant superintendent, and local superintendent. He is currently the Assistant Superintendent for Curriculum and Instruction for the Clermont County (Ohio) Schools.

Dr. Bradley is also an assistant adjunct professor in educational administration at the University of Cincinnati, a post he has held for eleven years. He has had numerous articles published, mostly on curriculum and rural education.

Foreword

THROUGH THE YEARS, curriculum leadership in schools has been a most neglected area. The task of curriculum development was placed on the overburdened shoulders of the principal and without sufficient allocation of resources. Curriculum development was a luxury; today it is a necessity.

Dr. Bradley's book fulfills an urgent need for a logical and systematic approach to curriculum development for those charged with this vital role. The processes outlined in this book are a result of years of refinement by Dr. Bradley in his position as curriculum specialist. This book will serve as the hub of your curriculum leadership toward successful curriculum development. It is a *must* in all educators' professional collections.

PALMER K. LOWE
Superintendent,
Felicity-Franklin School District
Felicity, Ohio 45120

About This Handbook

CURRICULUM LEADERSHIP AND DEVELOPMENT HANDBOOK is designed for busy principals and harried teachers whose environment consists of bells, buses, and kids— lots of kids. The world of these practitioners is often one of constraints and obstacles, with dialogue centering on "why we can't do that." Frequently, the principal's top priority is building management, and the teachers who are assigned curriculum responsibility are paid very little to participate in this crucial area. These facts alone lower the priority of curriculum work for them, and such is the reality of life for curriculum practitioners.

The other side of the coin is the textbook world of curriculum research, which focuses on what ought to be as opposed to what is. What's needed is for these two worlds to merge, thus changing and influencing each other. This is the ultimate goal of this book: to fuse the principles of the ideal with the "real" world of the practicing curriculum leader.

Who needs this book? Anyone who is currently a curriculum leader or is a participant in curriculum development. To determine how much you need this book, simply look over the following questions:

- Are you responsible for curriculum leadership and development but really don't know how to conduct curriculum development workshops?
- Would you like to make curriculum development a priority but don't know how to find the time?
- Are you supervising curriculum workers and really don't know what they are supposed to be doing?
- Would you like to get out from under the various curriculum theories and feel comfortable with a clear, concise, practical approach?
- Are you concerned about how to find the time to free teachers for curriculum development without hurting the instructional program?
- Would you like to know how to select teachers for curriculum work?
- Are you hazy about the differences between the assorted curriculum documents, such as courses of study and curriculum resource guides?

- Are you reluctant to plan curriculum change but would like to bring about improvement?
- Would you like a process to clarify curriculum decision making within a school district or buildings?

If you answered "yes" to one or more of these questions, then I urge you to read this book and begin implementing the suggestions immediately. Here are just a sample of the concepts and practical applications you'll find.

Chapter 1 lists and describes the six primary functions of the curriculum leader. It helps you *know what to do*.

Once you are familiar with your tasks, you must know how to go about implementing the curriculum process. This is explained in Chapter 2, in which many examples and forms are provided to help you develop the process.

Chapter 3 focuses on the two documents—the graded course of study and the curriculum resource guide—that are the most common products in curriculum development.

A curriculum leader has many functions that can be grouped into "expertise" tasks, role function tasks, communication tasks, supervisory tasks, and professional growth tasks. These five basic task groups are fully discussed in Chapter 4.

Making decisions about curriculum is the crux of any curriculum development. Chapter 5 helps you to make the right decisions and to follow through once those decisions are made.

Chapter 6 describes leadership styles and when they should be used.

Chapter 7 focuses on changing the curriculum after extensive study indicates that such change is needed. It is important to remember that tradition and change are a perpetual tug of war. To help you gather information in determining the traditions of a community, a fifteen-item "Tradition Identification Instrument" is included.

Finally, Chapter 8 explains how curriculum leadership and development come together to form a cohesive and working curriculum.

Throughout this book there are many forms, samples, and guides for you to use immediately in developing your skills as a curriculum leader.

LEO H. BRADLEY, Ed.D.

Acknowledgments

EVEN THOUGH THIS BOOK is largely based on my own study, research, and experience, it is in no way intended to mean that the ideas in the book are solely mine. Many of them evolved from dialogue with colleagues and others over the past two decades. These knowledgeable people ranged from educators to businesspersons to bricklayers. There are too many to name, and I would surely leave someone out.

However, there is someone who must be mentioned because of his significant contribution to the content of Chapter 3, which discusses curriculum process. Dr. John Hill, an associate professor at the University of Cincinnati, served as a consultant to me during the planning of the dialogue curriculum development model during the past seven years while I have served as curriculum leader for the Clermont County Board of Education in Batavia, Ohio. Dr. Hill's influence during the planning stage of this process was substantial.

The book *Management of Organizational Behavior* by Paul Hersey and Kenneth H. Blanchard was used as a reference in Chapter 7. The reference is, of course, noted. However, a footnote is not sufficient credit for the contribution that their book made to this text. The theoretical discussion from the section called "Motivational Research" is taken from the work of Hersey and Blanchard. The implications of the theory to curriculum leadership are my work.

Contents

Illustrations

CURRICULUM LEADERSHIP AND DEVELOPMENT HANDBOOK

chapter one

THE SIGNIFICANCE OF CURRICULUM LEADERSHIP

IT IS 9 A.M. An administrative team meeting is about to begin. The superintendent hands out the agenda. Item 1 is disciplinary problems on school buses. Item 2 concerns food on the cafeteria ceiling. Item 3 calls for a decision on whether or not students should be allowed to bring animals to school on the school bus. (This agenda item was prompted by a fifth-grader's bringing a pet snake to school in his pocket.) Numerous other items appear concerning boys' athletics, girls' athletics, negotiations update, and legal update. The last item on the agenda is stated "curriculum."

At 12:15, the superintendent pushes his chair away from the conference table, lights his pipe, turns to his curriculum director, and says, "John, it's all yours."

Curriculum Director: "Our agenda topic for today is how the quality of curriculum is affected by the principal. The research indicates that principals need in-service training in three areas: knowledge base, human development skills, and group process skills. The research also says that we must involve the teachers in these in-service sessions for the in-service sessions to have any positive effect. How can we proceed to get this in-service meeting rolling?"

Principal 1: "I'm willing to give up the last fifteen minutes of some of my staff meetings. We don't meet in December because of Christmas."

Principal 2: "Let's take care of it on the in-service day."

Curriculum Director: "This can't be done in one day. It will require an ongoing process."

Principal 3: "I know this is important, but it's 12:30 and I need to get back to my building. Besides, I'm hungry. Can't we talk about this next month?"

Superintendent: "Yes, we've been here more than three hours. That's long enough, John. We'll take it up later. Let's adjourn."

Curriculum Director: "Now wait a minute. I'm sick and tired of principals' never having time for curriculum. You don't need to be in your buildings all the

> time. We should be able to meet on curriculum matters anytime we need. That's why we have school anyway."
>
> *Principal 4:* "I have to go to the restroom."
>
> *Everyone:* "So do I. . . . " "Me, too. . . . " "Good idea."

Something is lacking in the preceding dialogue that is needed by all curriculum leaders—*knowing what to do.*

Just what are the functions of a curriculum leader? Although the list of functions would number in the hundreds if you compiled the literature presently available, here are some of the most common:

- To make contacts with the community to assist in the study of curriculum.[1]
- To be a resource person, a consultant to each staff in the various schools.[2]
- To help build a cooperative and permissive atmosphere conducive to work.[3]
- To coordinate and plan for the in-service education of all staff members, including teachers, principals, supervisors, and members of the superintendent's staff.[4]
- To facilitate curriculum improvement.[5]
- To provide for lay participation in curriculum improvement.[6]
- To help orient new teachers.
- To attend national, state, and local conferences on education and make reports of these conferences to local personnel.[7]
- To select textbooks.
- To train and direct curriculum consultants.
- To direct audio–visual education.[8]

But all functions are not equal in significance. Therefore, the effective curriculum leader must be able to identify and perform the most important functions. The following six functions should receive top priority from the effective curriculum leader:

1. Emphasize curriculum development: "How are we showing that curriculum development is important?"
2. Supply the necessary resources for curriculum development: "We'd like to try something; can you help?" Or, "We're thinking about doing this; can you help?" Or, "How do I get out of this mess?"
3. Provide philosophical direction to curriculum development: "What are we trying to achieve, anyway?"
4. Allow for continuity in curriculum development: "Are we all in this together?"
5. Bridge the gap between theory and practice in curriculum development: "That's the way it ought to be, but we can't do it, can we?"

6. Plan, implement, and evaluate curriculum development: "Can you have it ready by next Friday?"

Let's take a closer look at each of these functions.

EMPHASIZE CURRICULUM DEVELOPMENT

"How are we showing that curriculum development is important?"

Refer to the dialogue at the beginning of the chapter. This scenario reveals the absence of the two ingredients that must be present for curriculum emphasis to be happening in a school. First, this school system is giving only lip service to curriculum development. There is little honest commitment, as is evident by the fact that curriculum was last on the agenda, the superintendent's lack of interest in it, and the principals' attempt to deal with it in the least painful way. The curriculum director's comments indicate that he is not realistic in his expectations for curriculum development. His statement that principals could meet anytime indicates that he has not accepted the practical day-to-day obstacles that principals face. Therefore, both honest commitment and realistic expectations are missing in this setting. Needless to say, this administrative team is not emphasizing curriculum development.

A curriculum leader's efforts to provide emphasis on curriculum development is an attempt to reaffirm that the educational program's quality is the main priority of your educational goals. This is an assumption that is not verifiable in many school systems. But the effective curriculum leader will work diligently to establish the proper emphasis. If the curriculum leader doesn't treat curriculum development as the most significant aspect of schooling, emphasis will not be achieved.

If it is true that curriculum development is a piecemeal, haphazard process in many schools, the question persists as to how and why it continues. The answer lies in the nature of the educational program. Curriculum development exists whether it is planned or not. It may not be coordinated, but it exists. The teachers are teaching something, so that's the curriculum. Schools can operate without curriculum leadership and development—certainly not well, but they can operate. Other factors permit the classroom to function. Teachers are knowledgeable professionals who can make an educated guess at what the curriculum should be. Textbooks can be the curriculum. If there is no systematic curriculum development occurring, the curriculum is a combination of the teacher's knowledge and opinion and the textbook material, and even if the teacher "goofs" badly, there is a built-in failsafe: The student has a few more years to get "straightened out."

However, fixing previous mistakes is not the way to produce quality. That fact must be used by the curriculum leader to show the need for curriculum development and curriculum monitoring. Quality can be controlled and maintained only if horizontal and vertical curriculum continuity exists. Vertical curriculum continuity means that there is a systematic introduction and reinforcement of significant learning objectives

Kindergarten through Grade 12, thus eliminating useless repetition and damaging voids. This is where curriculum is developed.

Horizontal curriculum continuity means that all the teachers within a grade level or subject area are following the planned curriculum. This is how curriculum is monitored.

The curriculum theorist would place emphasis on vertical curriculum continuity and assume that horizontal curriculum continuity was present. The knowledgeable practitioner, attempting to provide curriculum emphasis, accepts the necessity of both curriculum development and monitoring; thus the need for both vertical and horizontal continuity.

These two necessary continuities can be present only if there is an emphasis on curriculum development. The fact that curriculum mistakes are not catastrophic is no excuse to tolerate indifference to curriculum development. Quality requires emphasis, and education deserves quality.

Where proper emphasis is being placed, the curriculum development process is a continuous one. The development of new knowledge and societal demands necessitate that curriculum development be a continuous process. This very logical fact would appear to make the continual revision of curriculum easy to promote. But it is not, because people who feel ownership to a product do not like to see it revised. Also, our capitalistic, competitive society teaches us to win and lose. We all prefer to win, but we can accept losing. What we have trouble with is not knowing whether we won or lost. And therein lies the problem with continuous curriculum development. You never win or lose but only produce the best document at a certain point in time, knowing that it will someday need to be revised. We are used to saying "that job is done." But in curriculum development, the job is never done—only temporarily established. Sometimes this has strange psychological effects on people. Two reactions are common, one positive and one negative. The positive is the fact that the product is not etched in stone and the teachers are aware that it will be revised in five years, which makes them willing to take risks. Sometimes these risks produce very positive results through new ideas.

The negative reaction is that the knowledge that their work will be revised sometimes makes teachers apathetic. This feeling is illustrated by the expression "Don't worry about it; it'll be changed soon anyway."

To achieve the proper emphasis on curriculum development, the proper balance between honest commitment and realistic expectations must be present. Also necessary is a positive attitude concerning the revision process. The presence of these two factors will produce continuous emphasis, which is the first prerequisite for quality curriculum.

SUPPLY THE NECESSARY RESOURCES
FOR CURRICULUM DEVELOPMENT

"We'd like to try something; can you help?" "We're thinking about doing this; can you help?" "How do we get out of this mess?"

These three questions represent the situations in which curriculum leaders are asked to provide human and material resources to the group in need. The group in need could consist of teachers, principals, or any other group involved in education. Sometimes they want help in determining what to do. At other times, they know what they want to do, but they want your help in proceeding. And of course, sometimes they're in a mess and want to know how to get out of trouble. Regardless of the reason for the need for resources, the curriculum leader can be a catalyst.

It is safe to assume that curriculum development is affected significantly by the curriculum leader's nature. This effect can be positive or negative. The nature of the effect will stem from the knowledge base, human development skills, process skills, and other human qualities of the curriculum leader. The curriculum leader is one of the significant variables, along with teachers, materials, finances, the board of education, and so on, that affect the quality of the school's curriculum.

Supplying the necessary resources for effective curriculum development requires two skills. The first skill is to provide the response or the material in an intelligent and informed manner. The second skill is to know how to locate and provide outside human resources and material when your own knowledge base and materials are not sufficient to meet the need. The wisdom to know when to use each skill is the key to supplying resources. No one expects the curriculum leader to be an expert in all curriculum fields. However, the curriculum leader is expected to know *that* and act accordingly. The "I don't know, but I'll help you find out" response is as positive as the "I know" response.

PROVIDE PHILOSOPHICAL DIRECTION TO CURRICULUM DEVELOPMENT

"What are we trying to achieve, anyway?"

Once upon a time a ship was sailing in the vast Pacific Ocean. The ship was sturdy, made of the best metal. It carried vast reservoirs of fuel and staples, more than enough to supply the crew for a long time. The crew was well trained and experienced. They all knew their jobs very well. The ship's officers were also competent and experienced. And at the helm was the captain, a man who had spent his entire adult life sailing the seven seas. He knew all the waters of the world. He had been through storms and near-mutinies. This ship was in good hands. There was only one thing missing on this giant, self-sufficient vessel: It had no destination. The captain knew the best routes to all the Pacific ports. The crew was ready to take them. But no one had set a destination.

As time passed, the ship remained strong structurally. There was still adequate fuel and staples. But something was happening to the people on board. The cooks began complaining, "I wouldn't mind peeling these potatoes if I knew where we were going, and how long it is going to take us to get there." The crew held an unofficial meeting on deck. One sailor said, "If we have no destination, what's the use in rushing to keep the ship moving? Let's just let her sit in the water. What's the difference?"

Even the captain grew bored. He had all this knowledge and experience, but he couldn't put them to use. So, he thought, maybe the men were right. Let the ship sit in the waters.

Soon this giant ship with all the resources and strength to carry out a successful voyage was "still in the water." The crew was stagnant. If only they had a destination. . . .

A lot of school systems are "still in the water" because they have no destination in curriculum. Like the giant ship, they are strong structurally. They have good facilities. Like the giant ship, they have adequate fuel and staples in the form of adequate finances that enable them to buy the materials and supplies necessary to provide quality curriculum. Their crew—the teachers—are well trained and experienced. Their captain—the superintendent—is experienced and knowledgeable in schooling. But they, like the giant ship, have no destination—that is, no curriculum destination. And, like the ship's crew and captain, this school's staff will also stagnate unless a philosophical direction that creates the educational mission and destination is determined.

It is the function of curriculum leaders to provide this philosophical direction. No one should have to ask, "What is the direction of that school's educational program?" It should permeate the system. The philosophical direction should influence the decision-making process. All school systems should know what it is, and how they can help reach the destination.

An example of philosophical direction in curriculum development is that many individuals participate in curriculum development. Curriculum development is not the sole prerogative of curriculum leaders, nor of scholars in the subject fields, nor of classroom teachers, nor of any other one group of educators or citizens. It is the obligation of all of these groups to participate. Curriculum is the one universal element of the school that reaches the entire school community. Therefore, it must be attended to by the total school community.

Whatever the philosophical direction may be, the significant factor is that there is a philosophical direction present, that it is clearly identifiable, and that it permeates every facet of curriculum development.

ALLOW FOR CONTINUITY
IN CURRICULUM DEVELOPMENT

"Are we all in this together?"

Of all the functions of a curriculum leader, providing curriculum continuity is probably the easiest to perform. It can be accomplished by adhering to two rules. First of all, when possible all curriculum developments should be Kindergarten through Grade 12 in scope. If properly done, Kindergarten through Grade 12 developments will ensure continuity. The second rule is that if a Kindergarten through Grade 12 involvement is not possible, then the grade level developing curriculum must have input from the other grade levels during the curriculum development. For example, if the intermediate grades (3, 4, 5) are working on curriculum, they must get input from the primary grades (K, 1, 2) and the middle grades (6, 7, 8). So long as we accept that learning is a continuous process, curriculum continuity will be a vital function of the curriculum leader. Isolated curriculum developments will occur without effective curriculum leadership, but coordinated developments will occur only when the curriculum leader provides for continuity.

BRIDGE THE GAP BETWEEN THEORY
AND PRACTICE IN CURRICULUM DEVELOPMENT

"That's the way it ought to be, but we can't do it, can we?"

Curriculum development is not a complete process until the curriculum is used in the classroom. This assumption implies that the planned curriculum is vital. If something is being taught, a curriculum is in existence, but it may not be the planned curriculum. Put in plain language, a planned curriculum not being implemented in the classroom is not the curriculum because it isn't being put to use. Needless to say, it is only through the planned curriculum that the curriculum leader can bridge the gap between theory and practice. If there is no planned curriculum, or if the planned curriculum is not being used in the classroom, then there is no theory of curriculum in existence.

However, if the planned curriculum exists, and if it is being used in the classroom, then the gap between theory and practice can be bridged if the curriculum leader can successfully overcome the obstacles, constraints, and facades present in curriculum development.

There are four obstacles to curriculum development that the curriculum leader must overcome. The first one is money. What is needed is "hard" money on a permanent basis. The amount of money needed will vary according to the size of the project. However, the size of curriculum development projects varies in direct proportion to the size of the school. Budgets for curriculum development also vary directly in proportion to the size of the school. Therefore, it is not the amount of money that is the significant factor. The important factors are, first of all, is the money "hard" money? This means: Are the funds a part of the regular school budget and not dependent on a federal or other types of special projects being approved? The second factor is, are the funds permanent? This means that the funds are not a part of some short-term contingent program. If the curriculum leader has "hard" money on a continual, not contingent, basis, this obstacle can be overcome.

The second obstacle is quality time for curriculum development. Quality time is the regular workday, 8:00 A.M. till 5:00 P.M. However, quality time is also defined as a day when curriculum development is the top priority for the participants. If teaching is also a part of the day, then curriculum development will not receive the concentrated, intellectual thought it needs. That obstacle must be removed if quality time is to be used for curriculum development.

The third obstacle to be overcome is the lack of commitment on the part of the school personnel. This lack of commitment occurs when the planned curriculum is not a significant part of the instructional program. Once the planned curriculum becomes the basis for instruction and evaluation, this lack of commitment will dissipate. The key is to connect the curriculum to the instructional program. Instruction always receives high commitment. When teachers see that the instructional program originates in the curriculum, they will become committed to the curriculum also.

The fourth obstacle to overcome is the lack of expertise. Curriculum development can't occur if the expertise is not present to properly plan, implement, and evaluate. The curriculum leader can remove this obstacle by making one of two responses when obstacles to curriculum development surface. One reply is "I can deal with that obstacle in this manner by. . . . " The second appropriate response is "I don't know the answer to that, but I know where to get help."

The constraints on curriculum development center on the repression of people's ideas and input. This frustration is often due to difficulty in fighting through the hierarchy or cutting through all the red tape. The curriculum leader must let people be heard. Hearing them out is more important than whether or not you accept their ideas. Too often curriculum leaders won't hear teachers out because of the fear that rejecting their ideas will be catastrophic to the teacher–curriculum leader relationship. Not true. What is catastrophic is to not hear people out.

Facades are smokescreens. The important skill in dealing with facades is to know how to recognize them and their true meanings. Following are two common curriculum development facades. The first part is what is said, and the second part is what it really means.

- "That's not important." ("I don't want to do it.")
- "I don't see the need for this curriculum development." ("I want to shut my classroom door and be left alone.")

The best way to deal with facades is to recognize them, but not call attention to them. To do so gives them credibility.

In school systems in which facades are present, their origin can usually be found in previous curriculum development practices that were unsuccessful. These failures tend to create facades so that the failure will not be repeated. As curriculum development becomes an important function of the school operation, the facades will disappear.

Begin to eliminate facades by accepting that having no curriculum development is better than a curriculum development that is not genuine but only a facade to meet some requirement or inspection, with no intent to guide the instructional program. Proceed with curriculum development only when it is meaningful, because then there are no legitimate reasons for people to utilize facades. But if they do, the curriculum leader has a right to expose and eliminate them.

PLAN, IMPLEMENT, AND EVALUATE
CURRICULUM DEVELOPMENT

"Can you have it ready by Friday?"

One of the dangers of being a curriculum leader is that people perceive you as somebody who won't work in the trenches. Somewhere in your curriculum leadership functions there has to be some tangible, visible work. When you plan, make sure that the legwork is done and that the routine matters are taken care of, so that workshop time can be spent on significant decision making. Be visible and involved during the implementation phase of curriculum you have helped plan. When things go wrong, be ready to assist in the problem solving. During implementation, be around. Don't disown your product or process when it springs a leak.

During evaluation, be willing to admit to errors, weaknesses, and shortcomings of your previous efforts. And last, but not least, set target dates and meet them. It makes curriculum development more organized and more tangible.

NOTES

1. Vernon E. Anderson, *Principles and Procedures of Curriculum Improvement* (New York: The Ronald Press Co., 1956), pp. 161–64.

2. Albert H. Schuster and Milton E. Ploghoft, *The Emerging Elementary Curriculum* (Columbus: Charles E. Merrill Books, Inc., 1963), pp. 539–40.

3. *Ibid.*

4. Glen Haas, "The Role of the Director of Instruction," *Educational Leadership*, November 1960, p. 101.

5. George M. Sharp, "Curriculum Coordinators Study Their Jobs," *Educational Leadership*, February 1955, pp. 464–66.

6. Ronald C. Doll, *et al.*, "What are the Duties of Curriculum Directors?," *Educational Leadership*, April 1958, pp. 428–30.

7. *Ibid.*

8. Alfred Papillon, "The Curriculum Directorship" (unpublished study, DePaul University, 1964), pp. 1–201.

chapter two

CURRICULUM PROCESS

CURRICULUM PROCESS IS the "heart" of curriculum leadership. This is the proof of the pudding! The curriculum development process separates the initiators from the doers. The curriculum world is full of good planners and initiators. Where curriculum development is falling short is in the implementation process.

The curriculum development process presented in this chapter can be applied to any subject area. It is consistent with the position that the curriculum leader is not looked to for content expertise. If the curriculum leader has to have content expertise, then schools are going to need a curriculum leader for each discipline. This is, of course, neither feasible nor desirable. However, the curriculum leader is looked to for "process" expertise. The curriculum leader is expected to plan, implement, and evaluate in such a way that the work of the content experts—the teachers—is facilitated.

The main characteristic of the dialogue model for curriculum development is that participants in the process are expected to rely more on dialogue to make decisions and less on individual preparation. Therefore, the participants do not deal with content decision making until they are in the actual development process with other participants. One rationale for the dialogue approach is that consensus is easier to reach if the participants do not begin with a fixed position. The dialogue approach gives participants the opportunity to listen to other views that will either contradict or support their viewpoints. Ownership is a very powerful psychological force. The dialogue approach will give participants the opportunity to acquire ownership of a group product. In the preparatory model of curriculum development, participants are asked to study individually and bring to the curriculum development process their own product. In the preparation model teachers develop an ownership of their work, thus making consensus more difficult to reach.

The assumptions upon which the dialogue curriculum development model is based are:

1. Teachers are the knowledgeable people about what content should be included in the curriculum.
2. Teachers can make decisions about scope and sequence.
3. Teachers can be credible consultants to their own faculties if they are trained in how to gather and assimilate staff input.

4. Curriculum leaders will provide the process expertise. Included in process expertise are:
   a. Selecting project models.
   b. Training teachers to gather staff input.
   c. Conducting curriculum development workshops.

As this chapter unfolds, it will become clear how these assumptions are applied to the dialogue curriculum development model. The steps in the curriculum development process are as follows:

1. Long-range planning.
2. Development of working model(s).
3. Three-phase development process.
   a. Planning workshop.
   b. Gathering staff input.
   c. Feedback workshop.
4. Publication and dissemination of documents.
5. Implementing curriculum in the instructional program.
6. Evaluation.

LONG-RANGE PLANNING

Establish a Curriculum Council

The makeup of the curriculum council is a most vital concern. Building principals, department heads, team leaders, and others in leadership positions should serve on the curriculum council.

Denying such individuals placement on the council is tantamount to saying that curriculum development is insignificant in the school organization. After all, people selected for principalships and department head positions are looked to for leadership in the educational program. Curriculum is the basis for the educational program. Therefore, these leaders should be on the curriculum council. Other reasons for this type representation are:

• Communication lines are already established through the organizational hierarchy; thus, if curriculum is a part of this communication, its effectiveness is increased.

• Supplemental contracts have been issued to these people, and these help legitimize curriculum development.

Functions of the Curriculum Council

Establish the sequence and review cycle for curriculum development. For example, a typical five-year cycle would look like this:

1980–81: Language Arts & Math   1985–86

1981–82: Science & Social Studies   1986–87

1982–83: Fine Arts   1987–88

1983–84: Developmentally Handicapped   1988–89

1984–85: Miscellaneous (all others)   1989–90

Choose Teacher Representation for Curriculum Development

There are five methods for choosing teacher representation for curriculum development; each has advantages and disadvantages. Following is a discussion of each method of selection and recommendations as to when it should be used.

VOLUNTARY

The advantages of the voluntary method are as follows:

- People who volunteer are interested in the project. The motives for this interest may vary. For example, the motive may be purely political; the teacher may feel that volunteering for curriculum work may impress the administration. Or the motive could be purely educational; the teacher may see the need for the curriculum development and wish to participate in its development. Regardless of the motive for the interest it can be assumed that a commitment is present.
- The use of volunteers is an open, democratic process.

The disadvantages of this method are that:

- Incompetents may volunteer, in which case the product will probably be of poor quality.
- Calling for volunteers seems to indicate that the position is not very important; the implication is that anyone is acceptable.

Recommendation for Use: Using volunteers for curriculum development is feasible when the group from which the volunteers come is made up of people comparable in ability. In other words, everyone is acceptable. In this situation, the volunteer method may be the most desirable one because it produces an interested participant. Also, it is democratic in nature, and the use of democratic processes when possible is usually good for rapport and morale.

ROTATION

The advantages of the rotation method are as follows:

- By rotating membership on curriculum committees, all possible participants can eventually be involved in curriculum development. The more that people are involved in curriculum development, the more they tend to use the curriculum documents produced by the curriculum development process. Therefore, rotating membership has the desirable effect of increasing involvement.
- Rotating eliminates the need for selection. That is a strength in itself because selection is often a controversial process.

The disadvantages of this method are:

- The biggest problem with rotating membership on curriculum committees is that there is little or no continuity. The degree of this problem will vary, but the problem will always be present. If rotation is used, the curriculum leader will have to keep in mind that two things will automatically occur: First, there will have to be a lot of attention given to the communication process to ensure continuity, and, second, the curriculum development process will take longer, because each time membership is rotated, there will have to be additional time set aside to bring new members up to date on the project.
- Rotating membership seems to assume that all eligible participants have equal ability to serve. Such an assumption may be erroneous.

Recommendation for Use: Rotating membership for curriculum development should be used when involvement is more important than continuity or efficiency. Always expect rotating membership to increase the time needed to achieve the goal. Rotation should be used when the eligible participants all have the ability to serve at an acceptable competency level. Or, to put it another way, the rotating membership will not prevent the development of an acceptable process or product.

EVOLVEMENT

The advantages of the evolvement method are as follows:

- Evolvement will usually produce the "true curriculum leader" from the group. If a group works together long enough, its members will recognize their qualities. One of the qualities that will be recognized is that of leadership, and it will belong to the "curriculum leader." The behavior of the group will indicate the confidence it has in this person. The group will use him or her in an informal manner as its representative.
- Cooperation from the group will probably be high because the group has chosen the "leader" or representative through its own processes. The selection has been an evolvement accomplished through the group's own informal structure

without guidance or coercion. Therefore, this is probably the truest "leader" that could be identified.

The disadvantages of this method are:

- The evolvement process takes too long to be feasible in any situation except a long-term one. Most of the time, the long term is too long for curriculum development projects.
- Leaders or representatives who have emerged are still without recognized authority. If you will recall, the gist of the discussion on the curriculum council was that the group should have representatives who have authority. If curriculum representation is allowed to evolve, the problem of establishing recognized authority is left unsolved.

Recommendation for Use: Using evolvement as a method of choosing teacher representation for curriculum development is feasible only as a first and unfinished step. It would be useful to use as a means of determining who the most competent teachers in curriculum development are. This information could then be used to choose teacher representation using one of the other methods of selection. If the evolvement process has been observed closely by the curriculum leader, the information gathered will improve the teacher selection process.

PEER SELECTION

The advantages of the peer selection method are as follows:

- By choosing their own representative, the members of the group will feel that they have more control over their own destiny.
- Since the group members chose their own representative, they are likely to cooperate with the project.

The disadvantages of this method are:

- The group may select representation for the wrong reasons—for example, because of friendship or even apathy.
- The peer selection method assumes that the group members know the kind of leadership and representation they need. In many instances, this may not be true.

Recommendation for Use: The peer selection process is highly recommended with the following conditions:

- The group must have maturity and experience.
- The group must be committed to the importance of curriculum development.

- The group members must be knowledgeable concerning the curriculum development. If they understand what kind of representation is needed, they can more intelligently choose a representative.

ADMINISTRATIVE SELECTION

The advantages of the administrative selection method are as follows:

- Administrative selection tends to legitimize a position, giving it significance. Since one of the problems curriculum faces is significance in the school power structure, administrative selection of teacher representation is helpful.
- Administrators should know who the best qualified person is.

The disadvantages of this method are:

- The administration may *not* know who the best qualified person is for the job. Or, perhaps more likely, politics will dictate rather than reason or intellect.
- As with all administrative decisions, this one may negatively affect group cooperation if the group feels the selection was based on politics rather than reason.

Recommendation for Use: Administrative selection should be used when peer selection is not feasible (see conditions necessary for good peer selection in the previous section). If administrative selection is used, be sure to treat the appointment as a significant one and therefore give it the time, energy, and thought that it deserves.

Assist the Curriculum Leader in the Selection of a Working Model

Members of the curriculum council should have knowledge of the components of the instructional and curriculum programs—textbooks, learning materials, philosophy, goals, and so on—that will be used as criteria to select the working model.

HOW TO DEVELOP A WORKING MODEL

A curriculum working model is a written curriculum document upon which a succeeding curriculum will be based.

One of the great "sins" that has been repeated over and over in curriculum development is the reinventing of goals, objectives, skills, and concepts over and over and over again. For too many years people have begun curriculum writing with a blank piece of paper. This is foolish when one considers the many sources of curriculum documents available in most fields. A more profitable approach is to begin with the work that has been done and then adapt it to your needs by additions, deletions, and revisions.

A working model helps produce the following positive attributes to curriculum development because it:

- represents a scholarly effort
- often represents a commercial or professional effort of national scope with a research base and field testing
- helps to establish consistency of language, which is important in curriculum documents and difficult to achieve when one is starting from scratch
- is usually written on a level of generality that provides needed flexibility.

In order to be used effectively, the working model must have the following characteristics. It should:

- have only one concept skill or objective per page (this makes deletion easy)
- have spaces to mark the scope and sequence
- have space to add any concepts, skills, or objectives that are desired.

Once the working model has been put together and the teacher consultants have been selected, the actual curriculum development is ready to begin.

A letter (see Figure 2.1) is sent to each teacher consultant after his or her selection and before the planning workshop.

Figure 2.1 Sample letter.

BASIN CITY PUBLIC SCHOOLS

September 29, 19—

Dear Course of Study Consultant:

Thank you for serving as your building representative to the course of study projects. Please find enclosed the schedule of the workshop dates.

To help you prepare for your role as consultant, the following information is provided. I hope that it will be helpful to you.

[1] Bring with you to the planning workshop textbooks and other curriculum materials used in your location. These materials will help you in both scope and sequencing.

[2] Your role as consultant involves three phases:
Phase A: Development of tentative graded course of study [scope and sequence of skills and concepts] in the planning workshop.
Phase B: Gathering input from your teaching staff on the tentative graded course of study.
Phase C: Finalizing the graded course of study at the feedback workshop.

[3] You will not be asked to write the objectives from scratch. You will be provided with a working model which you will add to, delete from, and revise.

[4] All workshops are held in the Basin City Board of Education Office.

I hope that you will find this a rewarding experience. I am looking forward to seeing you on your first workshop date.

Yours sincerely,

Leo H. Bradley, director,
Currriculum & Staff Development

LHB/al

Enclosures
Planning Workshop Agenda
Workshop Schedule (Planning and Feedback)

THE PLANNING WORKSHOP

The purpose of the planning workshop is to develop a tentative course of study using the working model and discussing strategies for gathering staff input. (See Figure 2.2 for a sample agenda.)

Figure 2.2 Planning-workshop agenda

```
 8:00– 9:45—Coffee and introductions—human development activities
 9:45–10:00—Presentation of working model
10:00–12:00—Development of scope and sequence
12:00– 1:00—Lunch (brown bag or off campus)
 1:00– 3:00—Continuation of scope and sequence development
 3:00– 3:30—Strategies for gathering staff input
```

Figure 2.3 shows the sample schedule of planning workshops for an entire school year.

The planning workshop is intense, and it brings together people who do not know one another. The task they are going to be asked to perform is a formidable one, with only limited time in which to perform the task set out. These three factors make it imperative that good planning and organization go into the workshop. In any of life's endeavors, first impressions are important. The planning workshop is the first workshop of the curriculum development process. Thus it will establish a level of credibility for the entire process. Many participants come into curriculum development with skepticism. A poor planning workshop will reinforce this skepticism. A good one will go a long way toward eliminating it.

Figure 2.3 Workshop schedule.

The following workshops will be held from 9:00 to 3:00 at the superintendent's office.

PLANNING WORKSHOPS
January 12, Primary (K–3), Language Arts
January 19, Primary (K–3), Mathematics
January 26, Intermediate (4–6), Language Arts
February 2, Intermediate (4–6), Mathematics
February 9, Middle School (6–9), Language Arts
February 16, Middle School (6–9), Mathematics
February 23, High School (9–12), Language Arts
March 2, High School (9–12), Mathematics

FEEDBACK WORKSHOPS
March 9, Primary (K–3), Language Arts
March 16, Primary (K–3), Mathematics
March 21, Intermediate (4–6), Language Arts
April 6, Intermediate (4–6), Mathematics
April 27, Middle School (6–9), Language Arts
May 4, Middle School (6–9), Mathematics
May 11, High School (9–12), Language Arts
May 18, High School (9–12), Mathematics

Note: Additional workshops or meetings could be held if needed.

Environment

Curriculum workshops should be held in comfortable environments. This means that the room has the following characteristics:

- comfortable work seats
- circular seating arrangement (if possible)
- tables with room for participants to spread their papers out
- good acoustics.

Also, make sure that appropriate refreshments (coffee, tea, donuts, and the like) are available. Name tags are also a good idea. They can be made by simply folding a paper so that it will stand on its own. Many people seem to resent name tags that they have to wear. The desk name tags are better accepted.

The planning workshop is now ready to begin. Let's now take a look at how each part of the agenda should be handled, beginning with the human development activities.

Human Development Activities

Please read this section closely. If you handle the human development activities incorrectly, you could destroy the entire curriculum development process. The activities needed for the planning workshop are very unsophisticated. Encounter groups or other "heavy" psychological settings are not needed. The purpose of the human development activities is to create a sense of openness, honesty, and trust among the participants. These three qualities must be present if good dialogue is to take place.

The first thing the curriculum leader should do is explain the reason for the human development activities. This will help create an atmosphere in which each individual will be open and honest and will trust enough to risk sharing opinions and positions.

Once the reason for the activities has been presented and discussed, the activities can proceed. Stay away from fantasy-like games that are a trial to the participants. Just do a few simple, realistic activities that give the following information about each person:

- name
- individual strengths in relation to curriculum development
- areas in which the individual will need help [or feels a little uncomfortable] in relation to the curriculum development to be undertaken
- Professional background
- Personal hobbies [something for the others to identify with].

These topics can serve as ice-breakers. Besides, you find out the human resources available by asking each individual to speak of his or her strengths. Don't think they won't share them. This structured setting makes it possible to do so.

The curriculum leader should participate in all the activities. Take the first turn. With respect to strengths, tell the participants that you will facilitate and provide process advice. With respect to "weak" areas, let them know that you are not the content expert. That is why they are there. People like to share their personal and professional strengths if they think others really want to know what they are. As curriculum leader, encourage them to tell you what you want to know.

Presentation of Working model

The only danger in using a working model is the possibility that it will be considered sacred by the teachers and therefore not really subject to change. In other words, the working model is what the powers that be (administrators, supervisors, boards, and so on) want, and the teachers are supposed to rubber stamp the model. Quickly state and demonstrate through your behavior that the model is not sacred in any way. Emphasize that the whole model is subject to change.

Once this danger has been averted, fully explain how the working model was chosen. Indicate the source or sources. Remember, a working model may be a combination of the strengths of many different sources. Explain why it was chosen. Indicate all the sources that were considered. Make sure that the participants know the purposes of the working model: (1) to use as a starting or focal point for the curriculum development, (2) to save time, and (3) to help provide consistency of language.

Scope and Sequence Development

Working with the scope and sequence is the "hard labor" of the curriculum development process. It is during this time that disagreements are hashed out and consensus is reached. It is time consuming and stressful. The curriculum leader must work to combat these two problems. The following strategies are helpful.

1. *Don't spend time agreeing to agree.* This is a luxury that would be nice to have. It is very pleasant to agree. It also allows the participants to reinforce one another, which is productive, but it takes time that the planning workshop schedule does not have. It may upset the participants at 9:30 A.M. not to be allowed to verbalize agreement extensively, but at 4:00 P.M. they will thank you.

2. *Accept silence to mean agreement.* In many curriculum subject areas, there is almost universal agreement on content. For example, in math, the multiplication tables are usually a part of the curriculum. When going through scope in these content areas, the participants will get tired of replying in the affirmative, which may include grunting. (Have you ever grunted for six hours?) Instead, let them speak when they disagree.

3. *Don't read each objective aloud in its totality.* For each objective, read just enough to keep everyone together. The first three or four words should be enough. Always indicate the number of the objective. Then let the participants read and think about it. Wait for someone to open the dialogue and, of course, allow the dialogue to lead to a decision.

4. *Emphasize that the curriculum decisions they are making should be based on what ought to be, not on what is!* Teachers have a tendency to base their decisions on whether or not a specific objective is currently being taught or is in the textbook they are currently using. Either alone is not justification to include the objective in the curriculum. The pertinent question is: Should it be taught? The curriculum leader must continually emphasize this point.

The following dialogue is presented to illustrate how the planning workshop should be conducted during the scope and sequence phase. The page of the working model being discussed is shown in Figure 2.4.

Curriculum Leader:	"Okay, let's look at LA 005. Show that you can follow oral directions. How about No. 1, pictures, etc.?"
Teacher Consultant #1:	"I think that is an essential Kindergarten objective."

Figure 2.4 Sample page of a working model.

LISTENING SKILLS		ESSENTIAL	IMPORTANT	NOT APPROPRIATE
LA 005	Show that you can follow oral directions.			
1.	Follow directions for drawing pictures.			
2.	Follow directions in making a copy of your own name from a model.			
3.	Follow directions in arranging pictures and objects in a predetermined order.			
4.	Follow directions for playing games.			
5.	Follow directions in marking worksheets.			
6.	Follow oral directions involving several steps.			

Teacher Consultant #2: "Oh, yes, everyone should teach that."

Curriculum Leader: "It has been suggested we accept subject objective #1 as essential. Is there anyone who disagrees or who would like to discuss it more?
(Silence)
"Okay, #1 is essential. Let's go to sequence. When is it introduced?"

Teacher Consultant #1: "It should be introduced at the Kindergarten and reinforced in Grades 1, 2, and 3."

Curriculum Leader: "Does anyone feel it shouldn't be introduced in Kindergarten and reinforced in 1, 2, and 3?
(Silence)
"Okay, that's it. #1 is essential, introduced in Kindergarten and reinforced in Grades 1, 2, and 3. Let's go to #2, Dictating sentence to teacher, etc. What do you think?"

Teacher Consultant #3: "We teach that."

Teacher Consultant #4: "We teach that too."

Curriculum Leader: "Do you think you should teach it?"

Teacher Consultant #3:	"Yes, I think it's excellent for teaching listening skills."
Teacher Consultant #2:	"Oh, yes."
Curriculum Leader:	"Okay, that information is pertinent because it speaks to what ought to be, not what is."
Teacher Consultant #1:	"I think it is essential, introduced at Kindergarten."
Curriculum Leader:	"Does anyone see this differently?"
Teacher Consultant #7:	"I agree it is essential. The kids love to do this."
Teacher Consultant #8:	"Oh, yes! For the students who have psycho-motor problems, print their name for them and let them trace it."
Teacher Consultant #1:	"For kids who learn best by feeling, cut the letters of their names out in sandpaper and have them trace the outline of the letters with their fingers."
Teacher Consultant #5:	"Fish gravel is good for some kids."
Curriculum Leader:	"All those are ideas that are great for teaching this objective. As a matter of fact, wouldn't it be great if we could have an in-service workshop on how to teach all the objectives? I wish we had the time for these kinds of discussions, but we don't. I'm afraid that today we are going to have to concern ourselves with the question of what ought to be taught—in other words, the curriculum. If, at the end of this course of study development, you feel that an in-service workshop is needed on how to teach the objectives, we will try to arrange it. I hope you will understand. "I take it everyone agrees this objective is essential for Kindergarten? (Silence) "Okay, let's go to No. 3, Arranging pictures, etc."

Blocking

There are some blockers to the curriculum development process that must be dealt with. Chief among these are the following stereotypes:

- Domineering participant: Talks too much, wants to control the process.
- Belligerent participant: Doesn't like the project and wants his or her attitude to permeate the whole group.
- Apathetic participant: Gives no evidence of commitment to the project.

- Nonverbal contributor: Has much to contribute but does not verbalize.
- Verbal noncontributor: Participates in an unintelligent manner.
- Impatient participant: Does not have the human development skills to function in the group process even though the knowledge base is there to do so.

Here are some strategies for dealing with these destructive workshop participants.

DOMINEERING PARTICIPANT

The key to dealing with the domineering participant is to control the domination without destroying the input. People who attempt to dominate meetings are troublesome, but they are also usually people of high commitment. Also, the fact that they are domineering does not mean that they are ignorant. Their input may be valuable. Therefore, the curriculum leader cannot resort to blunt reprimands that do control the domination but also destroy the input. One positive way to work with this problem is to ask for specific input from the other participants. For example, the curriculum leader may say, "Bob, how do you feel about objective number 110?" By specifically calling on participants other than the domineering one, the curriculum leader is reducing the problem. If the domineering participants interrupts other participants, simply say, "I'd like to hear the other people's opinion, then we'll hear yours. It is important that everyone participate in the discussion."

Care should be taken that the domineering participant doesn't wear down everyone to the point where it isn't worth it to disagree any longer. Do this by taking the time necessary for decision making on scope and sequence. The curriculum leader can also play a devil's advocate role with the domineering participant until the other participants are willing to oppose the domination.

Solving this problem requires patience and tact. Remember, as distasteful as the person might be, his input may be worth the trouble. Don't give up and lose the input—control the domination and keep the information.

BELLIGERENT PARTICIPANT

The belligerent participant is the most destructive of participants because negativism spreads quickly. You've no doubt heard the expression that one rotten apple can spoil the whole bushel. That is what can happen to your curriculum development process if the belligerent person is allowed to function for an extended period.

In dealing with this situation, the curriculum leader should act quickly. Attempt to find out the source of the belligerency. Some possibilities are that he or she:

1. was forced to serve against his will
2. thinks curriculum is not worth discussing
3. has had bad experiences with curriculum developments

4. wants to bring other issues into the meeting (instructional problems and the like)

When you find the source of the belligerency, confront it directly. The person who doesn't wish to be there can be told that he or she may leave. If he or she thinks that curriculum is useless, explain the reason for the curriculum process. Be positive. State that curriculum development is too important to be done by people who aren't committed. Stay on the offensive. Don't apologize if the person's experiences in curriculum were bad. That's not your fault. Neither is it relevant to the current situation. But most important of all, keep your cool. Don't become belligerent yourself.

After speaking thoroughly to the complaints, proceed with the curriculum development process. The ball is in the other person's court; he or she can leave or participate. However, he or she will no longer be permitted to permeate the meeting with negativism.

APATHETIC PARTICIPANT

The apathetic participant is both harmless and useless. Some attempt should be made to involve this individual in the process. If this proves unsuccessful, allow apathetic participants to behave as they wish. To give it continued attention with no results will hurt the working of the group. Do not ignore the participant; instead, leave the option for commitment open. The process may be so exciting that the individual will become committed.

NONVERBAL CONTRIBUTOR

The input of the nonverbal contributor is needed. The curriculum leader needs to act as the stimulus for this input. Ask the nonverbal contributor for the specific input that you know will be helpful to the group. *Do not* spend a lot of time encouraging him or her to "speak up." Obviously, this individual is of the type who speak mostly when spoken to. So, as curriculum leader, to ensure this person's maximum contribution, speak to him or her when you need to. At other times, let the nonverbal contributor pursue his or her own behavioral pattern.

VERBAL NONCONTRIBUTOR

The verbal noncontributor participates in an irrelevant manner. Every moment he or she participates is wasted time because the responses are unintelligent. The curriculum leader should, in a tactful and courteous manner, respond briefly to the comments of the verbal noncontributor and move the conversation on to something more productive. Do not allow the comments to become the basis for in-depth discussion concerning curriculum content. It has the potential to do so; that is why the curriculum leader should respond and move the conversation in a different direction.

IMPATIENT PARTICIPANT

The impatient participant does not possess the human development skills to function successfully in the group process of curriculum development even though the knowledge base is there to do so.

One hopes that the problems that this participant presents will be lessened by the human development activities experienced at the beginning of the planning workshop. However, if this doesn't do the trick, you might try the following strategy: Let the "impatient" make his or her points to you, and then you present them to the group. In this way, the input is saved. The assumption is being made that the curriculum leader has the human development skills needed to accomplish this task. Also, through your intercession, the group may be able to accept the ideas of the impatient participant even though they have difficulty dealing with the individual.

Note: Please keep in mind that the participant behaviors described in this section are pertinent only if the behavior is dominant and consistent. Almost everyone is occasionally domineering or belligerent or apathetic or nonverbal or impatient. However, if one or more of these behaviors are dominant and consistent, then the strategies discussed to facilitate the group process in curriculum development become necessary.

Also, keep in mind that the behaviors discussed are applied to a group setting and are harmful to the workings of a group. But since curriculum development is a group process, group behavior is the most significant kind of behavior to the curriculum leader. In almost all curriculum meetings, at least one of these overt behaviors will surface. The success of the meeting is often determined by how well the curriculum leader can combat the overt behavior.

Strategies for Gathering Staff Input

The purposes of this part of the planning workshop are twofold. First of all, it is an in-service activity for the teacher consultants on how to gather staff feedback. Secondly, it attempts to increase the chances that the staff input phase of the curriculum development will have some similar elements.

The basic concepts that should be covered in this session are:

1. How to plan meetings or work sessions.
2. How to conduct curriculum meetings.
   a. How to conduct human development activities.
   b. How to use the following types of small groups:
      Discussion
      Brainstorming
      Decision making
      Sifting
      Narrowing down

Discussion

Consensus

3. How to work with administration.

4. Emphasis that the most important thing is that all teachers *must be given the opportunity for input*.

The curriculum leader is responsible for providing the teacher consultants with enough copies of the working model to give to all teachers that the consultant must work with in the staff input process.

In discussing how to gather staff input, emphasize the following points:

1. The dialogue format established in the planning workshop must be continued during the input stage. If it isn't, the whole rationale for the process is destroyed.

2. Start with the building principal when attempting to schedule meetings for the purpose of gathering staff feedback.

3. In working with the staff, the teacher consultant should relay the thinking of the planning committee so the staff knows why the planning committee made the decisions it made. It strengthens the dialogue process.

Planning Workshop Rationale

This is a dialogue model as opposed to a preparatory model. It holds that better curriculum will be developed through the dialogue of knowledgeable consultants than would occur if each worked in isolation. It is a listening model in that it forces the teacher consultants to participate in curriculum decision making without prior knowledge of the working model content. Because of this, the teacher consultants cannot establish positions coming into the planning workshop. Therefore, the chances of good dialogue are improved because the participants have not had the time or opportunity to establish biases or positions.

Some people would say that the planning workshop would be more effective if the working model were sent to the teacher consultants before the workshops. In that way they would be better prepared to make curriculum decisions. However, it doesn't work that way. As a matter of fact, it creates poor curriculum decisions based on what is rather than what should be. Curriculum should be striving for improvement; it should not be a statement of the current state of affairs.

If the working model is sent out prior to the planning workshop, the teacher consultants will compare the model with what they are doing, not what they should be doing. To take time and money for curriculum development without an attempt to improve the curriculum is a foolish venture. The curriculum leader should make every effort to keep the thrust on improvement—on *what ought to be*. The dialogue model offers the best method of accomplishing what ought to be through curriculum improvement.

An underlying assumption in this curriculum development model is that the most knowledgeable teachers of the system will serve as the teacher consultants. If this is not true, the model is severely hampered. This is vital because the teacher consultants make some curriculum decisions that are not subject to staff feedback. They alone make the first alteration in the working model. These are very important decisions. If the teacher consultants are among the most knowledgeable teachers of the system, then the process will have a positive effect on the product. Needless to say, the reverse is also true.

The working model undergoes improvement through the following steps:

Revision 1: By teacher consultants at planning workshop.

Revision 2: By teaching staff during Phase #2.

Revision 3: By teacher consultants at feedback workshop based on their own beliefs, input from their staffs, and dialogue with other teacher consultants.

It should improve at each phase of development.

Figure 2.5 contains the directions as to how to use the working model. These directions would be given to the teachers at the beginning of the planning workshop.

Figure 2.6 contains one page of the working model as it would look to the teacher consultants. Figure 2.7 contains one page of the working model as it would look at the end of the planning workshop. Please notice that each objective has been marked either *essential*, *important*, or *not appropriate*. Also notice that each objective has been sequenced. By looking at Objective 6, you can see that it was marked *not appropriate*. Therefore, it is blotted out by a dark pen so that it cannot be read.

Gathering Staff Input

Assuming that the teacher consultants have been properly trained, the staff input phase should succeed if the following rules are carried out.

1. Allow four to eight weeks for the process. If the time allotted is too short, the teacher consultant may not be able to schedule the necessary time because of a busy schedule. If the time allotted is too much, it will be difficult for the teacher consultant to remember the details of the planning workshop, and the continuity of the process will be hindered.

2. Every teacher is given the opportunity for input. Every teacher may not choose to give input. That is not a problem. But all teachers must be given the opportunity to give input. To deny this opportunity will seriously jeopardize the chances of the document's being used by the teachers after it is finished.

3. The teacher consultant should work with the tentative course of study developed at the planning workshop. Under no circumstances should the original working model be used after it has been revised into a tentative course of study

Figure 2.5 A social studies working model.

WORKING MODEL
Directions to Teacher Consultants
SOCIAL STUDIES (S.S.)

This is a working model to assist in the development of an S.S. course of study.

On each page of this paper you will find objectives and sub-objectives within a major category of an S.S. program. Your task is to:

Step 1: Read and make sure you understand the objective and sub-objectives.

Step 2: Add to the list of sub-objectives any further objectives that you have or would want to have in your program. When you have written your additions on the pages provided, number each one and then proceed to step 3.

Step 3: Read each objective and sub-objective and decide (by placing a check in the appropriate column) whether the objective is Essential, Important, or Not Appropriate. (For those you have added, the decision is between essential and important.)

Definitions:

Essential: Means that the objective or sub-objective should receive top priority and must be in the course of study for the course of study to be complete. Essential objectives must be approved by all as essential.

Important: Means that the objective or sub-objective should be included in the course of study if time permits but will not replace the essential objectives and sub-objectives.

Not Appropriate: Means either of two things: (1) The objective or sub-objectives should not be included in a course of study. (2) The objective or sub-objective is not taught at these grade levels but may be appropriate at another level.

(Remember that only one check is appropriate for each objective or sub-objective. Do not check both essential and important.)

Step 4: Now look at the grade level columns. Your task is to check the grade level at which the sub-objective should be taught by introduction or reinforcement.

Definitions:

Introduced: At what time and in what grade level do you first deal with this sub-objective as an intentional part of the instruction? (When do you first try to teach the sub-objective?)

Reinforced: Means, in this paper, that by direct instructional activities you come back and go over or extend the learning about the sub-objective. It *does not* mean the informal and ongoing practice of a skill that would naturally occur in the ordinary activities of school. For instance, following oral directions is a listening skill that is practiced continually. We want to know where you intentionally introduce the teaching of the skill and where you repeat (reinforce), with actual instructional activities, the skill.

Step 5: When you have completed Steps 1 through 4 on major objectives, you have finished with that objective. Go to the next objective and begin with Step 1 again.

---

or curriculum resource guide. To do so would negate the work of the planning workshop and destroy the principle of continual revision, which is vital to the whole process.

Figure 2.6 A teacher consultant's working model form.

	ESSENTIAL	IMPORTANT	NOT APPROPRIATE	KINDERGARTEN	1ST GRADE	2ND GRADE	3RD GRADE
LISTENING SKILLS							
LA 005 Show that you can follow directions.							
1. Follow directions for drawing pictures.							
2. Follow directions in dictating a sentence to the teacher describing a picture, an object, or an experience.							
3. Follow directions in making a copy of your own name from a model.							
4. Follow directions in arranging pictures and objects in a predetermined order.							
5. Follow directions for playing games.							
6. Follow directions in marking worksheets.							
7. Follow oral directions involving several steps.							

4. The teacher consultant must realize that at the conclusion of the staff input process he or she must come to the feedback workshop with one position on the decisions to be made. It is important to realize that even if there is significant disagreement within the staff, he or she must come back to the feedback workshop with one position.

5. The teacher consultant must use dialogue in gathering staff feedback. To use checklists or other forms of nonverbal feedback would destroy the dialogue principle upon which the process is based. It would prevent the staff from hearing the rationale of the teacher consultants. Thus the staff members would be making their decision without the benefit of the expertise of these people who have already been identified as highly competent. If the teachers do not have the benefit of this information, they will make their decision in isolation, and this most often leads to a reaffirmation of what is, not what should be.

Feedback Workshop

The goal of the feedback workshop is to finalize the course of study or curriculum resource guide. All teacher consultants bring in a position based on their own expertise and opinions plus the input they have gathered from their staffs. It is highly recommended that consensus be used as the decision-making mode instead of majority rule. In curriculum decision making, editing the learning objectives through additions, deletions, and revisions is a good way to move toward consensus when disagreement is present. Also, flexibility is helpful. For example, degrees of acceptability—such as "essential" and "enriching"—are more desirable in curriculum decision making than a simple yes or no.

The same five-step process used in the planning workshop is used in the feedback workshop.

The feedback workshop has potential problems that are the opposite of those of the planning workshop. The feedback workshop comes at the end of the curriculum development process. Therefore, it is only natural that the teacher consultants are anxious to finish the project. The anxiety creates a rushed atmosphere, an attitude of "Let's hurry and get finished." This kind of atmosphere can produce sloppy work. The curriculum leader must make sure that enough time is devoted to this step of the process to ensure that additions, deletions, and other revisions are done properly. Remember, the feedback workshop is the last time the teacher consultants will be together. Don't leave any jobs undone. Don't permit any "railroad jobs" just to get finished.

PUBLICATION AND DISSEMINATION
OF THE CURRICULUM DOCUMENT

The steps to the dissemination process are as follows:

1. Publish enough documents for every teacher who is supposed to use it, plus one for each superintendent and the administrator who is concerned with the curric-

Figure 2.7 The same working model form after a planning workshop.

WRITING SKILLS

LA 010 Show that you can use grammatical principles correctly in written material.

	Skill	ESSENTIAL	IMPORTANT	NOT APPROPRIATE	ENGLISH I	ENGLISH II	ENGLISH III	ENGLISH IV	SPEECH & DRAMA	COMPOSITION/ CREATIVE WRITING	MEDIA	SHORT STORY, NOVEL, POETRY
1.	Recognize general nouns and specific nouns.	X										
2.	Recognize action verbs and forms of the verb *to be*.		X	X								
3.	Given a sentence with the verb in the passive voice, rewrite the verb in the active voice.		X		X	X						
4.	Given a sentence with a noun and its modifier(s) underlined, rewrite the sentence replacing the underlined words with a single noun that means the same thing but is more concise.		X		X		X					
5.	Given a sentence with a verb and its modifier(s) underlined, rewrite the sentence replacing the underlined words with a single verb that has the same meaning.		X		X	X			X			
6.	~~Recognize the following parts of speech in given sentences:~~ ~~1. noun 5. preposition~~ ~~2. verb 6. conjunction~~ ~~3. adjective 7. pronoun~~ ~~4. adverb 8. interjection~~											

    ulum or instructional program. Also, be sure to print enough so that sufficient documents will be on hand until the next revision.

2. Hold in-service meetings to explain to all teachers and administrators how to use the document. This in-service should include actual hands-on experience for the teachers and the administrators in using the document. The format should be thoroughly explained. The content should be skimmed so that teachers have an idea of what learning experiences are in the document. Also, in-service emphasizes that the document is important. If a curriculum document is simply handed out, the signal is received by teachers that here is another handout you may choose to use as you wish. Accompanying the dissemination with in-service emphasizes the importance of the curriculum's being implemented in the classroom.

IMPLEMENTING CURRICULUM
IN THE INSTRUCTIONAL PROGRAM

Of all the failings in curriculum development, the area of correlating curriculum and instruction is the most acute. Many curricula have no correlation with the instructional program. In fact, the curriculum planned is not the curriculum being implemented in the schools. However, it is not an impossible task. It must be done if curriculum is to reach its desired purpose of guiding the educational process. The following seven steps are recommended as a method of assuring correlation between curriculum and instruction.

STEP 1: IN-SERVICE OF CURRICULUM DOCUMENTS

    All curriculum documents do not follow the same format. Also, teachers are like other people in that they do not always read everything given to them. An in-service that explains how to use the curriculum documents in the classroom is the first step in assuring that the planned curriculum will be implemented in the classroom. However, the only purposes of this in-service are to create curriculum documents and motivate the staff to want to use the curriculum documents.

    Incidentally, if your curriculum documents are poorly written or have not had teacher involvement during their development, no amount of in-service will ensure their use in the classroom.

STEP 2: CLINICAL IN-SERVICE

    Most schools do Step 1 and stop. That won't get the job done. If it is followed up by clinical in-service, the chances of implementation are greatly increased. Clinical in-service means that teachers will use the curriculum document(s) (course of study and/or curriculum resource guide) in the classroom with students as a part of an in-service program. In other words, instead of an in-service that talks about how the curriculum documents should be used, the in-service consists of the teachers' actually implementing the curriculum in their instructional program. The usual length of this in-service is seven to ten days. See Figure 2.8 for a sample agenda of what the clinical in-service might resemble.

Figure 2.8 Ten-day agenda.

MONDAY, DAY 1, JUNE 19	
8:30–10:00 A.M.	• Introductions Registration Overview of Workshop
10:00–12:00 Noon	• Introduction of Clermont County Course of Study (Language Arts)
12:00–1:00 P.M.	• Lunch
1:00–2:00 P.M.	• Introduction of Clermont County Course of Study (Language Arts) Continued
2:00–4:00 P.M.	• Identifying Groups Group Development
TUESDAY, DAY 2, JUNE 20	
8:30–12:00 Noon	• Group Development and Decision Making
12:00–1:00 P.M.	• Lunch
1:00–1:30 P.M.	• Selecting Component of Course of Study
1:30–2:00 P.M.	• Learning Unit Planning
2:00–4:00 P.M.	• Learning Cycle Pre-Assessment
WEDNESDAY, DAY 3, JUNE 21	
8:30–12:00 Noon	• Human Development Activities for Kids Learning Styles
12:00–1:00 P.M.	• Lunch
1:00–4:00 P.M.	• Organizational Activities
THURSDAY, DAY 4, JUNE 22	
8:30–10:00 A.M.	• Planning for Teaching
10:00–12:00 Noon	• Instruction (Pre-Assessment)
12:00–1:00 P.M.	• Lunch
1:00–4:00 P.M.	• Grouping Kids Based on Pre-Assessment Planning Instruction Teacher Assignment Selecting and Organizing Materials
FRIDAY, DAY 5, JUNE 23	
8:30–12:00 Noon	• Instructional Strategies: Make It and Take It Workshop on Language Arts Materials
12:00–1:00 P.M.	• Lunch
1:00–4:00 P.M.	• Continued Unit Planning Selection of Learning Resources and Materials
MONDAY, DAY 6, JUNE 26	
8:30–10:00 A.M.	• Planning
10:00–12:00 Noon	• Instruction
12:00–1:00 P.M.	• Lunch
1:00–4:00 P.M.	• Criterion-Referenced Testing

TUESDAY, DAY 7, JUNE 27

8:30–10:00 A.M.	• Planning
10:00–12:00 Noon	• Instruction
12:00–1:00 P.M.	• Lunch
1:00–4:00 P.M.	• Critierion-Referenced Testing

WEDNESDAY, DAY 8, JUNE 28

8:30–10:00 A.M.	• Planning
10:00–12:00 Noon	• Instruction
12:00–1:00 P.M.	• Lunch
1:00–4:00 P.M.	• Follow-up Planning Diagnosing Academic Needs of Students

THURSDAY, DAY 9, JUNE 29

8:30–10:00 A.M.	• Planning
10:00–12:00 Noon	• Instruction
12:00–1:00 P.M.	• Lunch
1:00–4:00 P.M.	• Matching Curriculum Materials to Learners

FRIDAY, DAY 10, JUNE 30

8:30–10:00 A.M.	• Planning
10:00–12:00 Noon	• Instruction
12:00–1:00 P.M.	• Lunch
1:00–4:00 P.M.	• Follow-up Planning Post-Assessment Feedback

STEP 3: ENSURING PRINCIPAL COMMITMENT

Since it seems well established in education that the principal is the instructional leader of the building, he or she must be committed to seeing that the curriculum is implemented in the instructional program. Three things can be done to ensure that this step is fulfilled; however, the curriculum leader may not have control of these three processes, but, one hopes, will have some input. The least the curriculum leader can do is try to influence the people who make these decisions.

1. Recruit and employ principals who are curriculum oriented.
2. Include principals in curriculum in-service activities described throughout this book.
3. Make principals' commitment to curriculum implementation in instruction a part of their formal evaluation.

STEP 4: TEACHER EVALUATION

Teachers view their evaluation process (written form and follow-up conferences) as the "bottom line" on their role as teachers. The instrument used to evaluate teachers should contain a section on how well the teacher implements the curriculum in the classroom. This section should carry as much weight in the recommendation as any other section.

STEP 5: LESSON PLANS

Include in the lesson plan forms a place to indicate the curriculum source. For example, a blank space entitled "Course of Study Objective Number" could be placed on the lesson plan. By filling in the blank the teacher could convey the curriculum source of the instructional plan. (See Figure 2.9.)

Figure 2.9 Sample lesson plan sheet.

Teacher _____			
Grade	Grade	Grade	Grade
Subject	Subject	Subject	Subject
Course of Study Objective Number	Course of Study Objective Number	Course of Study Objective Number	Course of Study Objective Number

(MONDAY / TUESDAY grid)

STEP 6: CORRELATION OF TEXTBOOKS AND CURRICULUM DOCUMENTS
(course of study and/or curriculum resource guide)

Don't make the teacher choose between the textbook and the curriculum guide. The textbook will win every time. The following actions can be taken to avoid this problem.

1. Choose textbooks that most closely correlate with your curriculum documents.
2. If the textbook has been chosen and the curriculum is now being developed, use

the textbook in establishing scope and sequence. Don't let it dictate to you, but if it makes no difference, follow the format of the textbook in sequencing.

3. Make textbook correlation a part of the curriculum resource guide (discussed in more detail in Chapter 3).

STEP 7: CORRELATION OF STUDENT ACHIEVEMENT TESTING AND THE CURRICULUM

Develop criterion-referenced test items that measure the curriculum objectives. Then you are testing what you say you are teaching.

This is not to say you should not give norm-referenced tests. That is another decision that is based on other philosophical feelings. However, whether or not norm-referenced testing is done, criterion-referenced testing based on the curriculum should be done. If you assess student achievement based on the curriculum, the following cycle will be completed to ensure that the planned curriculum is implemented in the classroom.

Curriculum Planning
- Development of courses of study and curriculum resource guides

Curriculum Implementation in Instructional Program
- Principal commitment
- Lesson plans
- Textbook correlation
- Document in-service
- Clinical in-service

Curriculum Evaluation
- Teacher evaluation
- Principal evaluation
- Criterion-referenced tests
- Tests for student achievement

Curriculum: The Low-Priority Dilemma

Planning is necessary if effective curriculum is to exist. However, curriculum activities of some kind occur in the classroom with or without planning. If this were true of all areas of school administration and/or operation, curriculum might have a chance to climb the priority ladder. But it is not.

Consider the following: Envision a school system strapped financially to the point where only bare necessities will be met. A principal approaches the superintendent and says, "Would you sign this purchase order for $800 for the purchase of mathematics textbooks so that all the students will have a book?" The superintendent answers, "Is there a way you can make it through the year without the books? Couldn't the books be kept at school for two students to share? Perhaps the teachers could use other learning materials. Can you make do for the time being?"

The principal replies, "I suppose we could. It certainly isn't desirable. But I guess the teachers can run off dittos for assignments and we can make do." "Fine," says the superintendent, "when finances get better, we'll buy the textbooks. Oh, and incidentally, be sure to compliment the teachers on their improvising to make this undesirable situation work." The principal leaves, frustrated, certainly not satisfied, but determined to help in the financial crisis.

Soon thereafter, the transportation director enters the superintendent's office in a panic. In quick, slamming tones he cries, "Here, Boss, sign this purchase order quick. We had two carburetors and one motor blow today." The superintendent studies the purchase order. Ironically, it amounts to $800, the same amount he just refused a principal for curriculum material. "I'm sorry," replies the superintendent, "we're on an austerity budget, and this will have to wait." The transportation director lights his cigarette in such a way that the superintendent realizes the trump card is yet to be played. "Okay," says the transportation director, "that means that one of our buses will have to run a double route, which means that 120 students will be one hour late for school until the buses are fixed." "Isn't there a way to improvise?" asks the superintendent. "Sorry," replies the transportation director. "Kids can learn without textbooks and learning materials, or at least you can keep school going until money becomes available. But those buses just won't start without carburetors and motors." The superintendent signed the purchase order.

Immediacy: Present in almost all areas of administration, but not curriculum

An analogy can be made with the school administrative team functioning. If principals do not organize the lunchroom procedure properly, chaos will result. If they don't take care of discipline cases promptly, serious problems could occur. If they don't supervise and evaluate teachers, they will wish they had. If principals do not give enough attention to home–school communication, many people will notice. If the curriculum developments for the year are postponed or even canceled, they could go unnoticed. This might even be welcome in some quarters. Guess what gets short-changed in a pinch.

Immediacy is not the only cause of the lack of emphasis on curriculum development and implementation. Other causes include the lack of community awareness, lack of pay for teachers and/or administrative involvement in curriculum development, curriculum's not being a part of teacher evaluation, lack of consensus among professional educators concerning curriculum, and the perception of universal expertise existing in curriculum development when there is in fact little expertise in curriculum among both lay people and professional educators.

A good case could be made that the amount of emphasis in school programs is directly proportional to the degree of community awareness. Therefore, the curriculum cannot hope to compete in priority with sports, teacher evaluation, drama, and other areas unless community awareness of the significance of curriculum is raised to a comparable level.

CURRICULUM EVALUATION AND REVISION
USING THE DIALOGUE MODEL

The dialogue model for curriculum development presented in this chapter can also be used to evaluate the content and format of the curriculum documents (graded courses of study and the curriculum resource guide). The same assumptions upon which the developmental model is based apply to the evaluation process. They are: (1) Teachers are knowledgeable in curriculum content, (2) teachers can make decisions about scope and sequence, and (3) teachers can be credible consultants to their own faculties if they are trained.

The evaluation of curriculum documents should be based on their use in the classroom. A curriculum document should be evaluated every five years. Any revisions made in the document should be based on weaknesses discovered during the five-year implementation period. This is sufficient time for the classroom teachers, principals, and curriculum leaders to have discovered its strengths and weaknesses.

The process used to revise a curriculum document using the dialogue model varies slightly from the process used to develop an original document. Since any revisions are going to be based on the actual use of the curriculum document in the classroom, the gathering of this information should be the first step in the evaluation process. Therefore, the following five-step process is used for the evaluation and revision of curriculum documents.

STEP 1: STAFF INPUT AT LOCAL LEVEL

The teacher consultant will gather staff input on the current curriculum document in the following areas:

- Objectives: determine needed additions, deletions, revisions
- Sequencing the objectives: determine any needed changes
- Format: determine if any change in format or design is needed to make the course of study a better document (easier to use, more feasible, etc.)

STEP 2: PLANNING WORKSHOP

The teacher consultants will meet and develop a tentative revision of the curriculum document based on the information gathered during Step 1 and dialogue among themselves.

STEP 3: STAFF FEEDBACK

The teacher consultants will share the tentative revision with the local staff. If all local staffs are in agreement, the revision process will be considered complete. If there are still substantive differences, a feedback workshop will be held.

STEP 4: FEEDBACK WORKSHOP

The teacher consultants will meet and finalize the revision of the curriculum document based on the information gathered during all the preceding steps and dialogue among themselves.

STEP 5: REPUBLICATION, DISSEMINATION, AND IN-SERVICE ON THE DOCUMENT

Each time the document is evaluated, revisions should be made based on the results of five years of implementation. The following inputs are vital:

1. teachers' input as to value of contents
2. teachers' input on curricular void
3. teachers' input on curricular repetitions
4. teachers' input on curricular format
5. student achievement during the five-year implementation cycle
6. administrative input on content value
7. administrative input on curricular voids
8. administrative input on curricular repetitions
9. administrative input on curricular format.

VALUABLE STAFF DEVELOPMENT BY-PRODUCTS OF THE DIALOGUE CURRICULUM DEVELOPMENT PROCESS

The four most significant by-products of the dialogue curriculum development process are:

1. It can serve as the beginning of a faculty network for staff development.
2. It increases the teachers' knowledge of their subject areas.
3. It increases the teachers' knowledge of curriculum organization and development.
4. It produces curriculum leadership within the teaching ranks.

When teachers finish with the dialogue model process, they often ask that they be allowed to continue to meet. This request is a reflection of the satisfaction they find in discussing their academic field with their colleagues. In many cases, it is the first opportunity they have had to do so since graduate school. This interest can be used to build a faculty network for staff development.

Invariably, participation dialogue curriculum development increases the teachers' knowledge of their subject areas. This increased knowledge is usually in the form of instructional strategies to teach a concept, learning resources of which they were unaware, and philosophic or theoretical stances that differ from their own. In many instances, it will produce new insights and changes of opinion or position on the part of the teachers.

This increase in knowledge is helpful in two ways. First, the teacher will be more skillful in the next curriculum development. Second, the teacher will most likely be supportive of other curriculum development efforts because of his or her increased understanding of the need for curriculum development and the means by which it is accomplished.

Curriculum is not implemented in the office of the curriculum leader. Curriculum is implemented in the classroom. The dialogue curriculum development process will produce curriculum leadership within the teaching ranks. If the teachers are truly the decision makers in relation to content, and if the process meets their needs as well as the organization's, and if the product is quality, the teachers will be advocates of the curriculum.

chapter three

CURRICULUM PRODUCTS

GOOD CURRICULUM DOCUMENTS ARE the foundation for successful curriculum implementation. The documents are not an end in themselves, but are the means to an end. Having good curriculum documents will not ensure good curriculum. However, it is the first and vital step. Good curriculum documents serve the curriculum leader in the same manner that a good board of education policy book serves the school superintendent. You can't live on a foundation. But you can't build a house without one either.

Curriculum documents are tangible evidence of the existence of curriculum. In a sense, they are comparable to the building for the principal. They are the visible evidence that curriculum exists. For without them the curriculum leader is like a principal with no building or a teacher with no classroom. Therefore, the constant development and revision of quality curriculum documents, both graded courses of study and curriculum resource guides, should be a top priority for curriculum leaders.

This chapter will deal with two types of documents that are the most common products in curriculum development.

THE GRADED COURSE OF STUDY

The course of study is the official statement of what shall be taught in the classrooms of a school district. It is also a form of communication. As the official statement of what shall be taught, it represents an educational commitment on the part of the school personnel involved in its development and implementation. As a form of communication, it tells school personnel clearly and concisely what is to be taught in a given subject or area of study for a particular grade or combination of grades. It also conveys to all interested persons an accurate picture of what is currently being taught.

The course of study is primarily a working document that gives both structure and direction to the educational program. The philosophy of the subject area, as stated in the course of study, should be consistent with the stated philosophy of the school building and the school district. Goals and objectives should be those that best meet the needs of pupils of that district. Evaluation policies should be those that permit an accurate assessment of the extent to which objectives are met.

Although educators often use the terms interchangeably, a graded course of study is not a curriculum resource guide. The course of study and the curriculum resource guide have separate functions. The major differences between the two are as follows:

Course of Study	Curriculum Guide
1. Prescribes what is to be taught in a given subject or area of study.	1. Suggests how a given subject or area of study may be taught.
2. Is general in nature. Broadly defines the educational program in terms of philosophy, goals, and objectives.	2. Is specific in nature. Contains suggestions as to instructional aids, materials, learning experiences, teaching methods, and evaluation items.
3. Can be changed only by action of the Board of Education.	3. Is revised, altered, or amended as necessary at the discretion of school personnel.

If someone were to ask where curriculum development starts, most curriculum people would reply that it is in the graded course of study. Since this document is the basis and framework for all other curriculum development, it is vital that it be completed first. It is also vital that it be done well, for if it is deficient, other curriculum documents based on it will also be deficient.

Functions

The graded course of study serves multiple functions. First and foremost, it prescribes what is to be taught in a given subject or area of study. It is a legal document that is an official statement of the curriculum. In addition, it is the teacher's guide to instruction. Its content is used by the teacher in preparing and implementing daily classroom activities.

The course of study can be used to communicate to everyone concerned the intent of the school in relation to curriculum content.

Elements

A good graded course of study should contain all of the elements discussed in the following paragraphs. Although curriculum scholars may not agree as to the makeup of the elements as described here, their acceptance as necessary elements of courses of study is nearly universal.

Board of education approval and the signature of the chief administrator should always appear early in the document. In this way you will know whether or not documents are official. This element takes care of that need. (See Figure 3.1.)

Figure 3.1 Document approval for course of study.

BASIN CITY PUBLIC SCHOOLS

August 15, 19—

TO WHOM IT MAY CONCERN:

This letter is to certify that this graded course of study was officially adopted by the BASIN CITY BOARD OF EDUCATION on July 12, 19—.

Yours truly,

Thomas McCoy, supt.,
Basin City Schools

A *table of contents* needs to answer one question only. Can I find what I want quickly by turning to the table of contents? If the reader has to browse to find what is wanted, there is something wrong with the table of contents. (See Figure 3.2.)

An introduction should explain the purpose of the document and give a description or definition of its contents. It should also facilitate the reader's use of the document. (See Figure 3.3.)

Philosophy is probably the least used of any part of the document. However, that does not mean that it isn't important. The philosophy of the course of study should be consistent with the philosophy of the school. The user should be able to determine from it the broad purposes and beliefs of the school. (See Figure 3.4.)

Figure 3.2 Table of contents for course of study. (*Note:* Unless the document becomes too bulky, all courses of study should be K through 12. This promotes curriculum continuity. It also allows the teacher to better meet the curriculum needs of the students at the high and low extremes of achievement.)

Figure 3.2 *(cont.)*

Figure 3.2 *(cont.)*

Figure 3.3 Introduction to course of study.

I. Purposes of the Basin City Country Graded Courses of Study

1. to improve instruction within the local schools of Basin City.
2. to provide for continuity of curriculum within each local school
3. to provide the broad framework for the development of curriculum resource guides to supplement the graded course of study
4. to meet Section 3313.60 of the Ohio Revised Code, which requires that graded courses of study be prescribed by Boards of Education
5. to meet the policies and procedures established by the Ohio Department of Education in implementing Section 3313.60 of the Ohio Revised Code.

II. How to Use the Graded Course of Study

1. *Color Code**

Primary Objectives	K, 1, 2, 3,	Green
Intermediate Objectives	4, 5, 6	Gold
Middle and Jr. High Objectives	7, 8	Blue
High School	9, 10, 11, 12	White
	(by subjects)	

2. Scope

The Language Arts Course of Study groups objectives under the following skill areas (K–12)

Listening

Speaking

Reading

Writing

Grammar

Study

Communication

Language usage

Literary forms

Creative writing

Oral and dramatic interpretation

Analysis of media

- Each major objective is marked LA 105, LA 110, LA 115, and so on. A major objective represents a major growth point in student progress. Under each major objective are sub-objectives numbered 1, 2, 3, and so on, which lead the student to mastery of the major objectives.

- After each sub-objective you will notice an "E" or an "I". E stands for essential; I stands for important. The definition of each is as follows:

Essential: means that the sub-objective should receive top priority and must be in the course of study for the course of study to be completed. Essential objectives were approved by all Basin City Schools as essential.

Important: means that the sub-objective should be included in the course of study if time permits but will not replace the essential sub-objectives.

*Color coding enables teachers to quickly find their section of the course of study.

Note: If any sub-objective is marked "E" the major objective should be considered essential. If all the sub-objectives are marked "I" then the major objective should be considered important.

- Attention—Secondary Teachers: At the end of the English 10, 11, 12 courses of study, additional objectives are listed for those high schools that do not offer mini-courses or phase electives.

3. Sequence

After each sub-objective you will notice a column marked "Sequence." The grade indicated in this column is the majority feeling of the schools as to when the sub-objective should be taught by being introduced or reinforced.

Introduced: means at what grade level you first teach the objective as an intentional part of the instruction.

Reinforced: means that by direct instructional activities you repeat or extend the learning about the objective.

Note: This whole section is designed to provide flexibility.

Figure 3.4 Philosophy of course of study.

The Home Economics program is designed to prepare students for their future role as homemakers. We believe that the family is the basic unit of society in the economical as well as the sociological sense. Each student must be offered the opportunity for education in the skills, attitude, and knowledge necessary to help in the development of his or her potential as an effective member of the family and of the community. Homemaking is an intensely personal occupation. The program will help students to appreciate the cultural heritage inherent in the family tradition and customs, and also to use current information and technical knowledge to improve consumer skills, to manage effectively, and to seek out and appreciate the joys of living. The dual role of homemaker and wage earner is a reasonable expectation for today's student. Career opportunities in related areas are considered important in each unit of study in home economics.

Learning objectives take many forms. Some are behavioral in the strictest sense and thus highly measurable. Other objectives are much less behavioral in nature and less measurable. It is not the purpose of this book to explain and promote a particular type of learning objective. The vital point is that the objectives be written from the student's point of view. (See Figure 3.5.)

SCOPE

Every process that requires decision making seems to have decision areas that are difficult. In curriculum development, decisions regarding scope are the most difficult. Therefore, the more flexibility that can be used in scope decision making enhances the chances of reaching agreement. If the question in regard to scope involves a definite yes-or-no decision, stalemate often results. There are more things to consider than just whether or not the objective or concept is worthwhile. Another question that the determiners of scope must ask is, "Is there enough time to teach all the things that are deemed necessary?" The answer to that question varies according to the learners. Some learners can absorb vast amounts of curriculum. Other learners are capable of far

Figure 3.5 Learning objectives of course of study.

				Sequence
LISTENING SKILLS				
LA 005: SHOW THAT YOU CAN FOLLOW ORAL DIRECTIONS.				*Sequence*
	1.	Follow directions for drawing pictures.	E	K
	2.	Follow directions in dictating a sentence to the teacher describing a picture, an object, or an experience.	I	K
	3.	Follow directions in making a copy of your name from a model.	E	K
	4.	Follow directions in arranging pictures and objects in a predetermined order.	E	K
	5.	Follow directions for playing games.	E	K
	6.	Follow directions in marking worksheets.	E	K
	7.	Follow oral directions involving several steps.	E	K
SPEAKING SKILLS				
LA 010: SHOW THAT YOU CAN PRESENT IDEAS ORALLY.				
	1.	Describe in your own words how two objects or pictures differ.	E	K
	2.	Describe in your own words the probable reactions of persons in pictures and stories.	E	K
	3.	Express basic human needs.	E	K
	4.	Construct a story from a picture.	E	K
	5.	Construct story endings.	E	K
LA015: SHOW THAT YOU KNOW THE LETTERS OF THE ALPHABET.				
	1.	Identify uppercase and lowercase manuscript letters by name.	E	K–2
	2.	Given the alphabet, name both uppercase and lowercase manuscript form.	E	K
	3.	Identify the correct order of the manuscript letters of the alphabet.	E	K

Note: This numbering system allows for additional objectives without changing the number of existing objectives.

less. The curriculum writer is faced with the task of writing for all kinds of learners. Therefore, flexibility is vital. A feasible way to approach this problem is to categorize objectives as either required or enrichment learning.

If this is done, enough objectives can be included to sufficiently challenge the advanced learner. However, by classifying some of the objectives as enrichment, you are not condemning the learner with lesser ability to perpetual failure.

SEQUENCE

The course of study must deal with two types of teaching: introduction and reinforcement. The sequence of the course of study must indicate when concepts are introduced and when they are to be reinforced. To assume that objectives will be reinforced is an erroneous practice. Reinforcement is as vital as introduction in most cases, and more vital in others. The sequence should clearly indicate when objectives are introduced and reinforced.

CURRICULUM RESOURCE GUIDES

If classroom teachers are given a choice between having a graded course of study or a curriculum resource guide, they will take the curriculum resource guide every time. Why? Because it helps them do what they want to do best: *teach well!*

A curriculum guide is suggestive in nature. It is not a prescribed scope and sequence as is a graded course of study. It is an instructional aide. A good curriculum resource guide will include the following components:

1. correlation with the graded course of study
2. correlation with the textbooks and learning materials being used in the classroom
3. learning activities that can be used to teach the skills and concepts identified in the graded course of study
4. criterion-referenced test items to measure how well the students are demonstrating achievement of the skills and concepts identified in the graded course of study.

A discussion of each of these components is in order at this time so that the reader can understand their significance.

Correlation with Graded Courses of Study

All textbook and learning material correlation, all suggested learning activities, and all criterion-referenced test items should indicate the course of study objective from which they originated. By examining the sample curriculum resource guides found in this chapter, the reader can see how each page is marked to ensure clear understanding of the correlation.

Correlation with Textbooks and Learning Materials

One of the functions of the curriculum resource guide is to tell teachers where the objectives of the course of study can be found in the textbook and learning materials available to the teacher. Never make teachers choose between the textbook and the course of study. They will choose the textbook because it is the best teacher aid. Show them that by starting with their curriculum resource guide, they will be led back to the textbook and other learning materials at their disposal. Textbooks should not dictate curriculum; curriculum should dictate how we use textbooks. This happens only when the curriculum documents (graded course of study and curriculum resource guides) clearly connect the textbook content to the scope and sequence.

Suggested Learning Activities

Learning activities constitute the part of the curriculum resource guide the teachers like best of all. One of the aims of curriculum development is instructional help for the teacher. These learning activities are a boon for first-year teachers. They also give you the opportunity to tap the minds and resources of all your master teachers and make their expertise available to all your teachers. It is true that commercially published learning activities are available. However, to place them in one document within the classroom itself facilitates their use by the teachers.

Criterion-Referenced Test Items

Curriculum should be accountable. Schools should be able to confirm how their students are doing on *the school's curriculum*. Standardized tests nationally normed may or may not be measuring the school's curriculum. Criterion-referenced test items will measure the achievement of students in relation to the school's curriculum. The school that really wants to know specifically how its students are doing in relation to the school's curriculum has only two ways to find out:

1. develop and administer criterion-referenced test items, or
2. do an item analysis of the standardized test that you are using to see if your curriculum is being tested.

If the school does not feel that it has the resources (people, time, expertise, finances) to develop criterion-referenced test items for its curriculum, then an item analysis of the standardized tests being used is in order.

Sample Curriculum Resource Guides

Figures 3.6 through 3.17 are excerpts and samples from curriculum resource guides in language arts, mathematics, social studies, and science. It is hoped that examining these samples and excerpts will give the reader an idea of how the components of the curriculum resource guide look in an actual document. These figures illustrate:

1. how the curriculum resource guide is correlated with graded course of study objective
2. textbook correlation
3. learning material correlation
4. learning activities to teach objective
5. criterion-referenced test items.

The reader may also see how the curriculum resource guides correlate with the graded course of study also found in this chapter.

Just as with the exhibits on the courses of study, boxed notations are made to emphasize certain components or characteristics.

Figure 3.6 Sample curriculum resource guide: title page.

**CRITICAL SKILLS
CURRICULUM RESOURCE GUIDE
LANGUAGE ARTS** (K–12)

Critical Skills List
Criterion-Referenced Tests
Textbook Correlation
Learning Activities

BASIN CITY SCHOOLS

Figure 3.7 Sample curriculum resource guide: introduction.

PURPOSE:

This curriculum resource guide is intended to be an instructional supplement to the Basin City Language Arts Graded Course of Study. The Basin City Language Arts Graded Course of Study outlines a scope and sequence of skills and concepts (K–12). The graded course of study also classifies objectives as essential or important (see graded course of study for definitions). From the essential objectives the critical skills listed in this document were established. This Language Arts Curriculum Resource Guide is designed to help the classroom teacher with the instruction and measurement of these critical skills.

COMPONENTS:

This curriculum resource guide consists of the following components:

A. *Critical Skills.* These are defined as the most vital of the essential objectives found in the Basin City Graded Course of Study. They are based on the following four guidelines:

   1. *Is It Significant?*—That might be determined by (A) whether it is needed for further learning, (B) whether it is something an adult needs to know or is it something that when our students are adults, they will need to know, (C) whether a child of this age with "good schooling" would know this, (D) whether by the end of a school level such as primary or intermediate about 80 percent of our own students would know this, or (E) whether it applies to important things outside of school.

   2. *Does It Imply More Specific Learning?*—That is, (A) is it "big" enough or general enough to include more specific learnings, (B) if it has been learned, can we naturally assume that other, more specific learnings have been acquired?

   3. *It Is Teachable/Learnable?*—Under this guideline, some of the questions might be: (A) are learners at an appropriate developmental state to learn this? And (B) can it be taught in different ways? For instance, can it be taught in a concrete way for concrete learning? shown to a visual learner? presented intellectually to a symbolic learner? or applied to many real things?

The last guideline for a critical skills was the following question.

   4. *It Is Measurable?*—Some specific questions to help answer this question were: (A) Can it be

Figure 3.7 *(cont.)*

measured with paper and pencil test? (B) Can it be measured by learner performance? (C) Can it be measured by observing the learner? (D) Can it be measured by looking at student work samples? (E) Can it be measured by interacting with the learner?

A review of the course of study of goals and objectives using these guidelines resulted in a reduction in goals and objectives to the level of significance from essential to that of a critical skill. It was also determined that we would identify critical skills in the context of the learners who are taught in this country, in these schools. Finally, it was agreed that by critical skills, we did not mean minimal skills.

B. *Correlation with Textbooks and Learning Resources* The identification of critical skills then made possible the correlation of textbook series and commercial and teacher-made learning materials. This is done in chart form to identify pages within textbooks and printed materials, title, author, the publisher of media materials available, and identification of teacher-made materials. All series used by local school districts are recorded in the document.

C. *Criterion-Referenced Test Items* The guidelines for development of criterion-referenced test items were:

Does it truly test what the critical skill intends? Some practical ways to answer the true test (*validity*) guideline are suggested by these questions: If a student performs successfully on these items are you, the teacher, willing to say that the student has indeed learned the critical skill? If a slow student and a quick student both perform on these items without the constraint or limit of time, would you, the teacher, be willing to agree that both students had learned the critical skill?

The second guideline for developing or selecting a criterion-referenced test item is the *reliability* question. If a student could be tested several times with these items and had no memory of the past times, would your student likely perform in the same way on all these items?

The third guideline used was *objectivity*. Would teachers in your school likely use these items in assessment in a similar way? What directions might be included to increase the likelihood that these items would be administered in a similar way?

An additional area is included following the criterion-referenced test items that offered suggestions to the teacher about ways to assess through observation, performance testing, examining work samples, and interacting with the students. It was generally assumed that the majority of students could appropriately demonstrate their learning by paper and pencil testing. However, the performance test of learning is, without question, the best estimate of a learner's ability, implying an internalized, longer-lasting learned ability.

It is, of course, very time consuming to test each student through performance tests. it is very effective assessment but not very efficient when a single teacher may work with twenty-five to thirty students per class. Therefore, the optional assessment techniques other than paper/pencil tests are proposed as ways in which the teacher can work with a few of the students—those with special needs, those with learning problems, those who do not do well with paper/pencil items—or the mainstreamed child, or the child who needs remediation in a subject or topic.

D. *Learning Activities* For many of the critical skills, suggested learning activities are provided to assist the teacher with the instruction of the critical skill. It is never implied that these are the only ways to teach the skill.

Figure 3.8 Sample curriculum resource guide: flow chart.

CRITICAL SKILL NO. ___ 1 ___		
OBJECTIVE NO. (COURSE OF STUDY)	CRITICAL SKILL	LEARNING MATERIAL CORRELATION
		TEXTBOOK CORRELATION
LA 005	Show that you can follow oral direction.	No textbook is used to teach this skill.
Correlation with Course of Study	1. Follow directions for drawing pictures.	Developmental Learning Material Listening Tapes and Worksheets
	2. Follow directions in dictating a sentence to the teacher describing a picture, an objective, or an experience.	*Readiness Joy* by Joy L. Keeth—1975—P.O. Box 404, Napierville, IL 60540
From Course of Study	3. Follow directions in making a copy of your name from a model.	
	4. Follow directions in sequencing pictures.	
	5. Follow directions for playing games.	
	6. Follow directions for marking worksheets.	
	7. Follow oral directions involving several steps.	

Figure 3.9 Sample curriculum resource guide: language arts.

LEARNING ACTIVITIES ────────────────────────────────**CRITICAL SKILL NO. 1**

LANGUAGE ARTS

Kindergarten:

1. Following directions for shape and sequence.
2. Draw a picture of a story that has been read.
3. Learn to play "Simon Says."
4. Make up worksheets.

First Grade:

1. Tape a sequence of sounds for the children to identify.
2. Go on a sound walk and have the children identify sounds.
3. *Readiness Joy,* p. 216.

Second Grade:

1. Play the game "Simon Says." (The students should have mastered this skill by this grade. At this point, it is a teacher-observed activity.)

Figure 3.10 Sample curriculum resource guide: two activities.

JUST THE SAME

SKILL: Developing visual memory.

MATERIALS NEEDED: Worksheet A (one for each child) and crayons to color shapes.

PREPARATION: Have students cut the worksheet apart on the lines to separate the shapes.

ACTIVITY: This game can be for two players. Each student has a set of shapes. The first player arranges several shapes to make a design. The second player makes the same design. Then the second player closes eyes while the first makes some changes in the design. The second player changes own design to make it the same. Players change places and repeat the game.

VARIATION: The first player makes a design. The second player studies it. Then the second player closes eyes while the first removes something from the design. The second player tries to guess what is missing.

SHAPE AND COLOR

SKILL: Remembering an auditory sequence.

MATERIALS NEEDED: Worksheet A (two copies for each child), scissors, and crayons.

ACTIVITY: Children color worksheet and cut shapes apart. "Listen carefully to what I say: Large square, small triangle, small circle."

Do not repeat the sequence. Not put your pictures in that order. Will someone repeat what he or she has?

Continue with different sequences using two attributes (size and shape, shape and color, or color and size).

Figure 3.10 *(cont.)*

Increase the number of items in the sequence as the students are able to produce the sequences.

After practice with two attributes, use sequences with three attributes, such as small blue triangle, large red circle, small green triangle.

Note: These two activities are adapted from *Reading Fun and Games* by Libby Hollombe (Los Angeles: Rhythms Productions, 1979)

Figure 3.11 Sample curriculum resource guide: worksheet A.

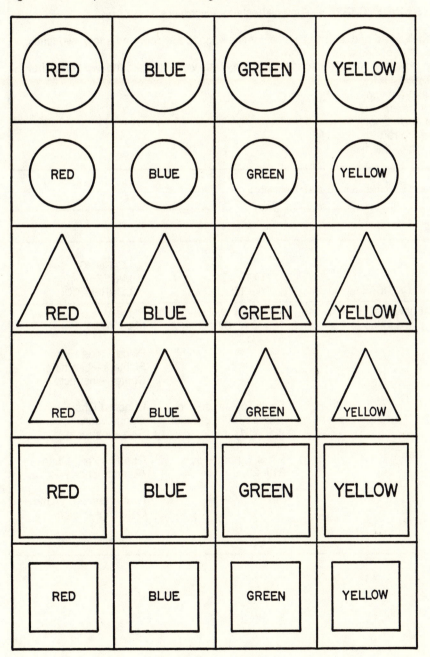

Figure 3.12 Sample curriculum resource guide: criterion-referenced test item.

CRITICAL SKILL #_____1_____   GRADE _____K–3_____

CRITICAL SKILL: Show that you can follow   4/6 _____
oral directions.   DEMONSTRATED ACHIEVEMENT

Student must get four of the six questions correct to have demonstrated achievement.

LISTENING SKILLS KINDERGARTEN: The child acts in accordance.
DIRECTIONS:
A. 1. "Go to the chalkboard and take four pieces of chalk; go to the door and knock two times,
       then run back to your seat and sit down."
   2. "Hop on one foot three times; clap once; go to the window and turn around two times; then
       hop back to your seat."
B. Draw pictures as I tell you:
   3. Draw a large circle.
   4. In this circle draw a square.
   5. Color the square red.
   6. Draw a line under the circle.

Figure 3.13 Sample curriculum resource guide: mathematics.

CRITICAL SKILL NO. _____1_____

OBJECTIVE NO. ___

(COURSE OF STUDY)	CRITICAL SKILL	TEXTBOOK CORRELATION	LEARNING MATERIAL CORRELATION
MA 010	Show that you can use place value to 99.	Houghton Mifflin—pp. 155–64, 167, 229–32, 310, 313.	Place Value Frame— Ideal #750
			Place Value Fire Fighters—Learning Center—Instructo
		Scott Foresman—pp. 163–64, 205–88; test 236, 251.	Hundred Chart— Flannelboard Sets—Instructo
		Silver Burdett—pp. 219–29.	One Hundred Chart— Allandin Charts—Ideal
			First Arithmetic Game— Counting—Dolch
			Numberite—Judy

Figure 3.14 Sample curriculum resource guide: two activities.

TENS OR ONES

PURPOSE: To give practice in working with tens and ones concept.

CONSTRUCTION: Cut 100 flash cards. Number these cards 1–100. Cut a 9″ × 9″ card for each student. Number the cards 1–9 randomly.

DIRECTIONS: Caller says a number such as 38. He then asks, "How many ones?" or "How many tens?" Students must respond to the verbal cue to tens or ones by placing a marker on the designated number. Caller then shows card to the players. First player to fill a row wins. This person becomes the next caller.

5	1	6
4	7	2
9	3	8

PLACE VALUE HOLDER

PURPOSE: Practice working on tens and ones.

CONSTRUCTION: Fold and staple an 8″ × 11″ sheet of construction paper to make two pockets. Label each pocket with the appropriate heading. Make two insert cards for each child of the numerals 0–9.

DIRECTIONS: Teacher displays some tens and ones. Child identifies the number card in each pocket. Then child writes the standard numeral. Teacher can also name number less than 100. Child identifies the number of tens and ones by putting appropriate numeral card in each pocket.

TENS	ONES

Figure 3.15 Sample curriculum resource guide: activity.

GOOBER GHOST & BENNY BAT
PLACE VALUE—ONES AND TENS

OBJECTIVE: Given a two-digit number the student will be able to identify the ones and tens columns.

STUDENT DIRECTIONS: Goober Ghost and Benny Bat want to go out and play tricks on everyone. Benny Bat has to know how many tens and ones are in each of Goober Ghost's numbers. Can you help? Match the correct ghost with each bat. Check your answers on the back.

TEACHER DIRECTIONS: Trace ten ghost patterns and ten bat patterns. Label each pattern with numbers similar to the ones on the ghost and bat.

Figure 3.16 Sample curriculum resource guide: activity pattern.

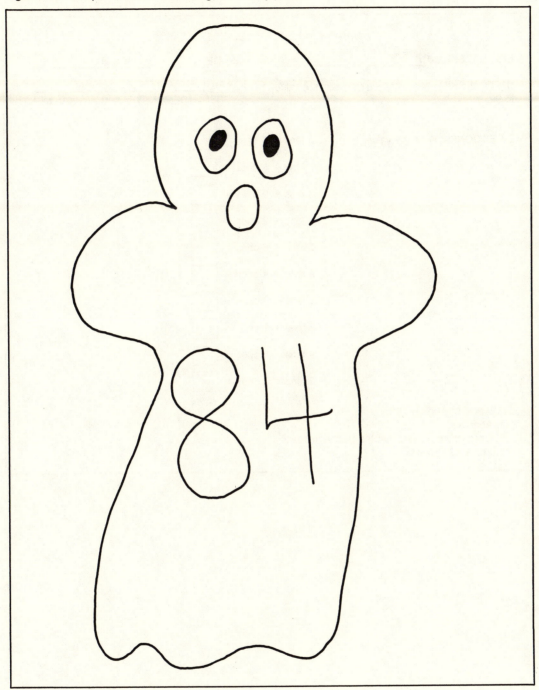

Figure 3.17 Sample curriculum resource guide: criterion-referenced test item.

CRITERION-REFERENCED TEST ITEM

CRITICAL SKILL #_____1_____   GRADE_____K–3_____

CRITICAL SKILL: Show that you can use place value
to 99.

$\dfrac{10}{8}$

DEMONSTRATED ACHIEVEMENT

DIRECTIONS: Write the value: 5 tens + 3 ones = ☐

7 tens + 5 ones = ☐

3 tens + 9 ones = ☐

4 tens + 2 ones = ☐

2 tens + 6 ones = ☐

6 tens + 4 ones = ☐

1 ten + 7 ones = ☐

8 tens + 1 one = ☐

9 tens + 8 ones = ☐

3 tens + 7 ones = ☐

ALTERNATIVE METHODS:
  1. Abacus
  2. Child writes number that the teacher reads
  3. Place value charts

chapter four

TASKS OF THE CURRICULUM LEADER

THIS CHAPTER IS DEVOTED TO a discussion of the various tasks that the curriculum leader performs in the day-to-day operations of the job. Each task will contain helpful hints on how to go about achieving the task.

The tasks are grouped into the following areas:

1. *"Expertise" Tasks:* Given to the curriculum leader because of his or her knowledge base.

2. *Role Function Tasks:* Perceived by others in the organization as the function of the curriculum leader.

3. *Communication Tasks:* Written and oral communications the curriculum leader must complete in order to perform the role function.

4. *Supervisory Tasks:* Performed in working with the personnel who assist the curriculum leader in organizing, developing, implementing, and evaluating curriculum.

5. *Professional Growth Tasks:* Necessary to maintain a knowledge base sufficient to exercise sound curriculum leadership.

"EXPERTISE" TASKS

Being an "Idea" Person

Curriculum leaders are expected to be creative thinkers who can keep new ideas available. Since curriculum leaders do not have as much direct supervisory responsibility as principals and superintendents, they are expected to have time to think and study to produce useful ideas for the school administration to consider. All healthy organizations need to be constantly considering new ideas. Good curriculum leaders will give this task sufficient attention.

Helpful Hints

1. Have some practical, feasible, possible ideas as well as far out, idealistic,

difficult-to-implement ideas. Otherwise, you may be perceived as a useless, ivory-tower idealist.

2. Read, read, read. Keep up with the literature of the field.

3. Don't always speak off the top of your head. Present some of your ideas on a more academic or intellectual basis.

4. Don't be in a hurry to respond when someone asks you for some ideas. Creative thinking sometimes takes some thought and time. A good idea is worth waiting for. Quick lips eventually become suspect.

Meeting with Publishers and Salespersons

Meeting with publishers and salespersons is a task that helps keep the curriculum leader current on the newest publications in the field. Sometimes, their visits are untimely. However, the information they bring is often helpful. Therefore, it is a task that should be performed.

Helpful Hints

1. Since you have to see many of these people on a continual basis, your memory will not be able to store all the information received. Therefore, create a filing system that will enable you to quickly locate the file when you need to do so.

2. Discard any sales information that you know has no future value for you. Otherwise, in a year, your office will look like the center of the annual paper drive.

3. Let salespeople know how much time you expect to spend with them when they come in. Take no more or no less time then necessary.

Being a Resource Person for Administrators, Teachers, and Other School Groups

Being regarded as someone with expertise includes being regarded as someone who knows where to go to get information. Other members of the organization will look to you when they need this information.

Helpful Hints

1. Be selective in supplying resources. If you feel that a resource is questionable, don't give it. In this way you are acting as a screening device and thus eliminating poor resources. This saves time for the other administrators.

2. If you are gathering resources for someone, do it completely enough so that the person does not have to get more information before acting. If he or she does, the value of your activities will be questioned.

ROLE FUNCTION TASKS

Answering the Mail

Answering the mail is something that all educational administrators do—not just curriculum leaders. It is worthwhile discussing, however, because it can take up too much of the working day if not handled properly.

Helpful Hints

1. Don't do it during "prime" time. Do it when you can't do other, more important tasks—for example, after teaching personnel have left for the day or before they arrive.
2. Let your secretary respond to routine correspondence.
3. Let your secretary open the mail. It saves time.

Setting Up In-Service Meetings

Setting up in-service meetings requires that you consider many factors carefully before acting. Keep foremost in mind that you are interested in ensuring maximum participation, high motivation, good environment, and proper timing. These four components are vital to successful in-service meetings.

Helpful Hints

1. The morning is the best time to hold in-service.
2. Provide, if possible, at least two weeks' notice to the participants.
3. Provide a comfortable, attractive environment, including food and drink.

Setting Up College Classes

Setting up college classes is becoming more significant in staff development for curriculum improvement. It is one of the major ways to motivate teachers to get involved in curriculum development.

Helpful Hints

1. Hold the class as close to the school as possible.
2. Cut the red tape as much as possible; for example, register on site.
3. Know who the professor is going to be. If you do not approve of the university's choice, ask for input into the professor appointment. If the university officials refuse to allow your input, inform them that if you do not approve of the professor you do not wish to have the class offered. No class is preferable to a poor

class. Always keep in mind that you may wish to have these teachers participate in future in-service. One bad experience can drive them away. Always, consider the long-term consequences.

Developing Curriculum During the Summer

Summer is obviously a good time to develop curriculum. It presents some obstacles or at least special considerations that must be addressed. The helpful hints are directed toward these special considerations.

Helpful Hints

1. Give teachers at least two weeks to recuperate from school before starting the summer workshops.
2. Find an air-conditioned building.
3. Don't enroll the teachers for summer curriculum activities in the middle of the winter. Everyone seems interested in summer curriculum activities in January. But many things seem to happen by June that change personal plans. More realistic planning can occur if enrollment is done in March, April, and May.

Developing Budget Proposals

Budgeting procedures for curriculum development are the same as for other departments except that there is usually a larger percentage of funds needed for printing and consultants.

Helpful Hints

1. Do your homework. Know what curriculum development expenditures such as consultants and printing cost.
2. Stand up for curriculum. Just because it is not "nuts and bolts" expenditures does not mean that it isn't important. Learn how to explain curriculum in tangible terms so that you can promote the necessary funds to properly carry it out.

Long-Range Planning

In view of the fact that the curriculum leader is the administrator with the K–12 administrational perspective of the school, he or she is looked to for long-range planning. A good curriculum leader should have the next five years planned.

Helpful Hints

1. In relation to long-range planning, the following information is needed:
   a. What are the goals, objectives, and activities for the next five years?

   b. What are the target dates for each goal, objective, and activity to be carried out? (See Management Forms in Figures 4.1 through 4.3 that can be used to record this information.)

2. Communicate and recommunicate the long-range plan on a continual basis. Otherwise, it becomes lost in the day-to-day operations.

Figure 4.1 Goal statements.

	NAME	
	FINISH DATE	RESPONSIBILITY
1. The Basin City Schools shall revise the existing courses of study in the field of art.	1. Aug. 1, 1985	Curriculum Director
2. The Basin City School shall implement competency based education in language arts K–3.	2. Jan. 30, 1985	Principals
3.	3.	
4.	4.	
5.	5.	
6.	6.	
7.	7.	
8.	8.	

Figure 4.2 Planning guide.

NAME _____		
GOAL STATEMENT #1. The Basin City Schools shall revise the existing courses of study in the field of art.	Start Date: Finish Date:	Aug. 1, 1984 Aug. 1, 1985

OBJECTIVES:	FINISH DATE	RESPONSIBILITY
1. One teacher consultant from each grade level will be chosen.	1. Sept. 15, 1984	Principals
2. Teacher consultants will revise the scope, sequence, and format based on dialogue and staff input.	2. May 1, 1985	Teacher Participants
3. The revised course of study in art will be published and disseminated to all art teachers.	3. Aug. 1, 1985	Curriculum Director
4. _____	4.	
5. _____	5.	
6. _____	6.	
7. _____	7.	
8. _____	8.	

Figure 4.3 Activity planning sheet.

NAME		
OBJECTIVE #2. Teacher consultants will revise the scope, sequence, and format based on dialogue and staff input.	Start Date: Target Date:	Sept. 15, 1984 May 1, 1985

MAJOR ACTIVITIES:	TARGET DATE	ACTUAL RESPONSIBILITY
1. Teacher consultants will meet with their principal to arrange a time for grade level meeting.	1. Oct. 1, 1984	Principals
2. Teacher consultants will meet with grade level teachers to discuss strengths and weaknesses of existing art course of study.	2. Oct. 15, 1984	Teacher Consultants
3. Teacher consultants will meet in a Planning Workshop to tentatively revise the existing art course of study.	3. Nov. 10, 1984	Curriculum Director
4. Results of the Planning Workshop will be shared with all staff.	4. Jan 30, 1985	Teacher Consultants
5. Teacher consultants will meet in a feedback workshop to finalize revised art course of study.	5. May 1, 1985	Curriculum Director
6.	6.	
7.	7.	

Conducting Workshops and Other In-Service Sessions

The only part of the staff development program that most teachers see is the workshops and other in-service sessions. Therefore, it is the part of the program upon which they base their evaluation of in-service. You, the person responsible for this program, must make sure that in-service activities reflect competence.

Helpful Hints

1. Never "wing" it. Plan, plan, plan. The only thing that should happen on the day of the in-service is the in-service itself.
2. Never assume that the equipment and material you need will be provided by someone else if you are going to a building to do an in-service. Take your own back-up equipment (extension cords, adapters, screens, and so on) just in case.

Orienting Teachers

If first impressions are important, then teacher orientations too are very important. Keep in mind that the curriculum leader is an educational leader. Therefore, he or she should communicate the philosophy, goals, and objectives of the educational program of the school.

Helpful Hints

1. Don't brainwash or indoctrinate the staff. Instead communicate and inform the staff.
2. Don't use an "ivory tower" approach. Show them that curriculum is in the mainstream of the learning program.

Interviewing Teachers

Principals have a set of priorities when interviewing teacher candidates. For example, they will try to determine if the candidate will be able to maintain discipline. Superintendents will try to determine if the teacher will be good at communicating with parents, because that relationship affects the public opinion of the school, which is vital to the superintendent. The curriculum leader should ask questions that determine whether or not the candidate understands and accepts the role of curriculum in the school.

Helpful Hints

1. The student-teaching experience usually leaves significant impressions upon the student teacher. When interviewing, probe into this experience and determine if the person has developed an educational philosophy compatible with that of the school you represent.

Selecting Teachers for Curriculum Development

When selecting teachers for curriculum development, look for people with skill in content knowledge, communications, and writing. These are three skills needed for curriculum development.

Helpful Hint
1. Use teachers who will be willing to say to other teachers that curriculum development is important.

COMMUNICATION TASKS

Surveying Teachers

Surveying teachers gives the curriculum leader an idea of what they are thinking. This task is important if the curriculum leader is interested in the teachers' opinions. Since the teachers are the implementers of the curriculum, the leader should be very interested.

Helpful Hints
1. Don't ask for information you do not intend to use.
2. Don't ask for information without giving feedback on that information.
3. Make your survey instruments as simple to answer as possible.

Collecting and Summarizing Feedback

A report containing teacher feedback is one written communication that is likely to be read by the teachers because it is telling them what they said. Of course, that is of great interest to them.

Helpful Hints
1. Do not editorialize on the feedback.
2. Combine similar responses in one category so that the feedback is easier to read and understand.

Speaking on Curriculum and Instruction Topics

Making addresses on relevant topics is one of the most difficult tasks that curriculum leaders are called upon to perform. It is also one of the most important. What makes it difficult is the vastly different audiences that you are asked to address.

Helpful Hints
1. Avoid the use of educational jargon. Examples of educational jargon to be careful with are:
   a. input
   b. feedback
   c. feasible

    d. relevant

    e. criterion referenced

    f. alphabet soups (there are too many to name)

    g. complex process

2. Be human—be warm, with a sense of humor.

3. Don't act as if curriculum were the most vital topic in the universe. It isn't.

4. Be brief. Curriculum is not the subject on TV talk shows. It is not commercial.

Disseminating Research

One of the dangers of public schools' curriculum operation is that it becomes what Miller[1] refers to as practice-practice, or monkey see, monkey do. Anti-intellectualism is alive and well in schools as well as in other places in society. It is the curriculum leader's task to combat the tendency toward monkey see, monkey do or practice-practice. The curriculum leader should maintain a theory into practice stance of the school. One of the ways to do this is to read the latest research and disseminate the findings to the other administrators and teachers in the community.

A word of caution should be given to the curriculum leader concerning the task of disseminating research. Do not assume that you are determining what teachers should read, or that you have to interpret it for them also. The dissemination of the research is meant to motivate them to keep up with the educational literature in their field and to assist them with suggestions and information. Theoretically, teachers should do this on their own. Practically speaking, however, teachers can use help in this vital area. The effective curriculum leader will provide this assistance. If done properly, teachers will appreciate the effort.

Helpful Hints

1. Disseminate the research in understandable English. Interpret the results so as to make them more readable. However, don't change the meaning of the research findings.

2. Disseminate research findings that will be helpful to the administrators, teachers, or laypeople in their jobs. In other words, put research into action.

3. Include annotated bibliographies of the latest literature and research. This will indicate to the teacher the kinds of materials available. The teachers can then choose books and articles that are of interest to them. It also indicates that the research being disseminated by the curriculum leader is only a small portion of what is available. There is also the hint that teachers should keep up with the research and literature. This is, of course, the main reason the curriculum leader should be involved in this task.

Writing Memos

Memos are written daily. They should clearly contain the intent of the memo. They should be brief. Bear in mind that they are impersonal in nature.

Helpful Hints

1. Use forms that require mostly checks (this saves time).
2. Memos are too impersonal to be used on important matters.

Preparing Agendas

Agendas should be sent out prior to meetings. An agenda has two purposes: It provides guidelines for the meeting, and it helps the persons attending the meeting to come prepared. They cannot do this if they haven't received the agenda. (See Figures 4.4 and 4.5.)

Figure 4.4 Agenda sheet.

BASIN CITY SCHOOLS

September 7, 1984

TO: Curriculum Leaders

FROM: Lance Hawkins, assistant superintendent, Curriculum/Instruction, Basin City Board of
          Education

RE: Curriculum Meeting

  Date: September 20, 1984
  Time: 9:30 a.m.
  Place: Administrative Office

AGENDA

1.   Secondary Reading Course of Study Distribution
2.   Course of Study Revisions for '84-'85 school year
      Art
      Music
      Physical Education and Health
3.   Competency-Based Education Program

      •   In-Service for Primary Staffs
      •   Field Testing for International Language Arts
      •   Implementation and monitoring for Primary Competency-Based Education
      •   Principal communication to public

4.   Membership Items

Figure 4.5 Information sheet to assist you in preparing for the meeting.

1. Competency Testing—Suggested Procedure

    Step #1: Identify competency items from courses of study (Primary, Intermediate, Middle, High School).

    Step #2: Develop or identify test items to measure each competency item.

    Step #3: Develop or identify the methods to be used to determine the ability level of each student.

    Step #4: Field test the competency items; revise field test until community is satisfied.

    Step #5: Initiate competency at local level.

    A. Time Line for Suggested Procedure

1984–85	1985–86	1986–87
Step #1	Step #4	Repeat Step #4
Step #2		or Initiate
Step #3		Step #5

    B. Decisions That Need to be Made in Order to Carry Out the Suggested Procedure.

    Decision #1: What subject areas will be included in the competency exam?

	Yes	No
Language Arts	_____	_____
Math	_____	
Social Studies	_____	_____
Other: _____	_____	_____
_____	_____	_____
_____	_____	_____

    Decision #2: Should we develop our own test items or identify them from commercial sources?

    Decision #3: How many levels of competency testing will be used?

    Suggested Levels: Exempt all educationally handicapped students who are not being mainstreamed into the regular curriculum.

    Level #1: The Minimum Competency

    Descriptors

    - For students with 80 to 100 I.Q.
    - Required for graduation
    - Survival-skill oriented
    - Vocationally oriented
    - Parallels general and vocational curriculum

Figure 4.5 *(cont.)*

Level #2: The Potential Competency

Descriptors

- For students with 100 and above I.Q.
- Not required for graduation
- Desirable for post-secondary education success
- Parallels college prep curriculum

Decision #4:	How will students be placed at each level?
Decision #5:	At what grade levels will the competency test be given?
Decision #6:	Who decides on competency items?
Decision #7:	Who decides on how intervention will be implemented?
Decision #8:	Who decides on Decisions #1 through #7?

Helpful Hints

1. Put informational topics at the beginning of the agenda.
2. Always leave a portion of the agenda for topics of interest to the members of the group. (In other words, don't totally dominate the agenda.)

SUPERVISORY TASKS

Curriculum leaders are often assigned the task of supervising special projects (federally, state, or locally funded) or special area educators such as counselors or reading or media specialists.

Since these people are almost always in a building and thus under the jurisdiction of a principal, special problems result. As curriculum leader, keep in mind that you are in charge of the program and the personnel of that project when they are working *on their project*. At other times they are the responsibility of the building principal.

Helpful Hints

1. Stay in close communication with the principal.
2. Evaluate the project personnel and communicate the evaluation to them. Keep in mind that your evaluation should center only around the project that you, as curriculum leader, have been assigned. Do not infringe upon the principal's evaluation areas.

PROFESSIONAL GROWTH TASKS

A curriculum leader must stay current on curriculum trends and research. Five good ways to do that are to:

- read the current literature
- attend professional meetings
- visit other curriculum leaders
- learn to listen
- stay in touch with the local universities.

Helpful Hints

1. Put some time aside each day for professional reading.
2. If 10 percent of what you hear and see at a professional meeting is worthwhile, it is worth your time.
3. Don't be an "island" unto yourself. Share with your colleagues. Learn from them.
4. Read more!

CONCLUSION

In relation to curriculum leadership, tasks are not an end in themselves. They are one means through which the curriculum leader works with curriculum process. If the curriculum leader is an efficient task performer, it will enhance his or her overall effectiveness by providing more time for the more significant functions such as process, decision-making, and product.

Tasks are often mundane. But if you do them well, perhaps your job won't be mundane because you won't always be bogged down with tasks. Then you can be the creative leader you want to be.

NOTES

1. Van Miller, "The Practical Art of Using Theory," *Organization and Human Behavior*, edited by Carver and Sergiovanni (New York: McGraw Hill, 1969), p. 133.

chapter five

CURRICULUM DECISION MAKING

THE SIGNIFICANT GOALS THAT a school district should strive for in curriculum decision making are:

1. Integrating curriculum and instruction.
2. Keeping curriculum in the power structure of decision making.
3. Clarifying decision-making roles in the curriculum process.

INTEGRATING CURRICULUM AND INSTRUCTION

"Curriculum cannot stand alone. It is useful only if it is implemented in the instructional process." Now that sounds like an assumption that any school district would accept, doesn't it? The fact of the matter is that curriculum and instruction are not integrated well in many school districts. There are decisions made about curriculum and there are decisions made about instruction. But there are not enough decisions made that include both curriculum and instruction.

Most curriculum decisions center on the development of curriculum documents. Questions relating to design, format, and content are examples. There are also many decisions made about instruction. Most of them concern how individual teachers are performing in the classroom. Decisions are made about the quality of the teachers' questioning skills, listening skills, small group techniques, and like details.

What is needed are curriculum decisions that tie the curriculum in with the instructional program. This implies that curriculum is more than a printed document: It is a living process involving people. Therefore, the decisions involved with it concern people. A common word for people in organizations is *personnel*. Therefore, curriculum decisions should involve personnel, and personnel decisions should involve curriculum.

Decisions made about personnel are central to the evaluation process. Curriculum should enter into the staff evaluation process in two ways. First of all, the evaluation of teachers should include how well they are implementing the planned curriculum in the classroom. Secondly, the evaluation of the principal should include how well he or she is supervising and leading the implementation of the curriculum in the classroom.

By using the evaluation process, school districts can indicate through their actions that instruction is a vital component of curriculum. It is indicating that curriculum is a "living" part of the school program. And most important, it will tie curriculum and instruction together.

KEEPING CURRICULUM IN THE POWER STRUCTURE OF DECISION MAKING

One of the major problems that curriculum has is its inability to stay in the power structure of the decision-making process. In many schools, involvement in curriculum decision making is not necessarily considered prestigious. As a matter of fact, it is sometimes considered a nuisance. This sad state of affairs is illustrated by the fact that many schools are without a formal decision-making structure for curriculum. A second indicator is the haphazard ways in which teachers are chosen for involvement in curriculum development. It often comes down to who is willing or, worse yet, whose turn it is.

A definite decision-making process should be established for all facets of curriculum. This decision-making process should include personnel that represent the decision-making power structure. Department heads, assistant principals, principals, and central office personnel concerned with curriculum should be included in the decision-making process. It is of limited value to create curriculum councils or other organizational mechanisms that are not in the decision-making power structure. If you do, it will have little or no effect on curriculum decision making. Therefore, as curriculum leader, see to it that the people who form the decision-making power structure of the school are involved in the curriculum decision making.

CLARIFYING DECISION-MAKING ROLES IN THE CURRICULUM PROCESS

There is often a lack of clarity in curriculum decision making. This lack of clarity takes two forms: conflict and ambiguity. Conflict in curriculum decision making centers on curriculum leaders and principals. In too many instances, both are claiming primary responsibility for the same decisions. Ambiguity in curriculum decision centers mainly on teachers who are not sure who makes curriculum decisions. Thus they do not know with whom to communicate on curriculum decision making.

The nature of the relationship between principal and curriculum leader lends itself to conflict and ambiguity. Both positions work with the same personnel—basically, teachers—to achieve the goals of their programs. If both positions are working with the same program and personnel, sharing and close working relationships are implied.

To ensure a positive working relationship among teachers, principals, and curriculum leaders, a clear decision-making structure must be maintained. The approach and strategies must be used to eliminate the decision-making conflict and ambiguity between principals and curriculum leaders. Strategies must also be used to reduce the ambiguity that seems to exist among teachers as to who makes curriculum decisions.

Decision-making clarity in curriculum can be achieved by identifying the significant curriculum decisions, identifying the decision makers, and deciding how to communicate the decisions.

FOUR VITAL QUESTIONS
ABOUT DECISION-MAKING ROLES

The following four questions are vital to an organization in relation to roles in curriculum decision making:

1. What decisions need to be made to ensure that the curriculum can be properly planned, implemented, and evaluated? (*Note:* The assumption is being made that good curriculum planning, implementation, and evaluation are a goal of the school and that commitments are being made to achieve the goal.)
2. Who is primarily responsible for making the decision?
3. Are there secondary decision makers? If so, who are they?
4. Who communicates the decision to all the people who are affected by the decisions?

Let's now discuss each of the four questions in more detail, beginning with the question of what are the vital decisions to consider.

> *Question 1:* What decisions need to be made to ensure that the curriculum can be properly planned, implemented, and evaluated?

There are ten major decision areas for curriculum decision making. They are:

1. long-range planning
2. home–school communication
3. planned change
4. curriculum evaluation
5. in-service staff development
6. instructional staff personnel
7. budgetary
8. curriculum committees
9. department heads
10. team leaders

For a curriculum program to function properly, the curriculum leader must input into all these decision areas.

Question 2:   Who is primarily responsible for making the decision?

Question 3:   Are there secondary decision makers? If so, who are they?

Needless to say, the principal is also involved with decisions regarding these ten areas. Therefore, the decision-making roles that each performs in these areas must be clarified so that all involved with the curriculum process are clear as to who decides what.

Keep in mind that *who* makes the decision is not nearly as important as *clarity* among the staff as to who makes the decision. Success in curriculum decision making can be accomplished through a strong principal–weak curriculum leader organization or vice versa.

In an attempt to help school systems clarify the curriculum decision-making process, a discussion of each of the ten decision areas is presented here with recommendations concerning how each one should be handled. These recommendations are based on my experiences and are meant to be a source of information for the reader. Bear in mind that they do not represent the only way to make these decisions. The intent of this section is to emphasize that these decision items must be clarified if a school system is to have a good curriculum decision-making process. Who winds up as the primary decision maker is secondary to how well the process is classified and communicated.

LONG-RANGE PLANNING

1. Who determines problem areas for curriculum study?
2. Who assigns priorities to problem areas for curriculum study?
3. Who decides the long-range curriculum time line?

Recommendations

- The curriculum leader should establish *the long-range curriculum time line*. This is one of the major reasons to have a curriculum leader position. The curriculum leader should have the total perspective necessary to make these decisions.

- Determining problem areas in need of study could come from either the principal or the curriculum leader.

- Assigning priorities to problem areas should be the decision of the curriculum leader. Once again, the curriculum leader has the K–12 perspective necessary to assign priorities. The principal may be knowledgeable about his or her own building's curriculum problems but is not in a position to see the overall K–12 picture.

HOME–SCHOOL COMMUNICATION

1. Who decides the public-relations program for curriculum development?
2. Who decides what news items are to be released?
3. Who approves the content of the news items that are released?
4. Who decides who shall interpret curriculum at public meetings?
5. Who decides on how to gather feedback from the community on curriculum?
6. Who decides on how to report pupil progress to parents?
7. Who determines which community members/parents will be invited to participate in curriculum studies?

Recommendations

- The keys to good news releases are timing, writing style, and good content. Above all, a good curriculum leader should be a good writer.

- Principals should sometimes interpret curriculum at public meetings. For the curriculum leader to always perform this task implies too much central-office ownership of curriculum.

- Gathering, analyzing, and disseminating feedback is a time-consuming task. It is better not to do it than to do it haphazardly. Give the task to the person who has the knowledge and the time to perform the function well.

PLANNED CHANGE

1. Who decides if a course of study shall change content?
2. Who approves the content of a new course of study?
3. Who decides the instructional organization?
4. Who decides which teachers are assigned to new instructional/curricular programs?
5. Who decides what elective academic experiences will be included in the curriculum in addition to the state requirements?
6. Who approves additions to or deletions from the curricular program?
7. Who decides how to evaluate the success of the teaching of a new curriculum?
8. Who carries out this evaluation process?
9. Who directs the implementation of new curriculum?

Recommendations

- Instructional organization should reflect continuity (K–12).
- Curriculum content change should be handled by the curriculum leader to ensure consistency of language, design, and format.

CURRICULUM EVALUATION

1. Who decides how to evaluate the ongoing curriculum process (planning, developing, implementing)?
2. Who carries out this evaluation?
3. Who approves the selection of textbooks and learning materials?

Recommendations

- Lean on the curriculum leader heavily in this area. Curriculum leaders should have expertise in curriculum evaluation.

IN-SERVICE

1. Who decides the content of orientation meetings?
2. Who decides what types of activities will be used for in-service sessions?
3. Who decides teacher and staff assignment procedures for in-service activities?
4. Who evaluates the in-service program?
5. Who appoints teachers to curriculum committees?
6. Who decides topics for staff in-service?
7. Who decides the in-service schedule for the year?
8. Who is responsible for consultants or speakers for in-service programs?

Recommendations

- The principal should assign teachers to curriculum committees.

INSTRUCTIONAL/STAFF PERSONNEL

1. Who decides if the instructional methodology is in line with the instructional philosophy?
2. Who decides if the teacher is pursuing subject-matter content as prescribed by the curriculum guide?
3. Who decides on ways to group pupils?
4. Who evaluates the classroom performance of teachers?
5. Who selects teachers for appointment?
6. Who decides assignments of staff?

Recommendations

- This is pretty much a principal decision-making area. The curriculum leader should be given input in two aspects: (1) Are teachers using instructional methodologies in line with the instructional philosophy? and (2) are teachers pursuing the subject matter prescribed by the course of study?

BUDGETARY

1. Who determines the amount of money needed for implementation of a new curriculum?
2. Who determines building budget allocation toward curriculum projects?

Recommendations

- This is another area that requires a K–12 perspective. Therefore, the curriculum leader should be given decision-making leadership.

CURRICULUM COMMITTEES

1. Who coordinates and directs the work of curriculum committees K–12?
2. Who coordinates and directs the work of building curriculum committees?

Recommendations

- It may seem logical that the curriculum leader should direct K–12 committees and the principal should direct building committees. However, the function is extremely vital to the success of curriculum development. If it is not properly conducted, the quality of the curriculum will be seriously affected (see Chapter 2). The curriculum leader should perform both these functions for two reasons. First of all, consistency will be achieved. Second, the curriculum leader should have expertise in facilitating curriculum committee work.

DEPARTMENT HEADS

1. Who appoints department heads?
2. Who evaluates the performance of department heads?
3. Who decides if the department head is to be retained as department head?
4. Who decides how the administrative evaluation will be communicated to the department head?

Recommendations

- These are obvious principal decisions. The curriculum leader needs to be consulted about the performance in curriculum areas.

TEAM LEADERS

1. Who appoints team leaders?
2. Who evaluates the performance of team leaders?
3. Who decides if the team leader is to be retained as team leader?
4. Who decides how the administrative evaluation will be communicated to the team leader?

Recommendations

• These are obvious principal decisions. The curriculum leader needs to be consulted about the performance in curriculum areas.

Figures 5.1 through 5.3 show an instrument that a school system can use to determine the perceptions of the people in the schools (teachers, principals, curriculum leader, superintendent, central office administrators) about who makes the decisions or who should make the decision. By using the instrument, schools can determine on which decision items there is clarity as to decision making. It can also be determined where there is conflict in decision making, and areas where there is ambiguity in relation to decision making will be revealed. The results of the instrument can then serve as the basis for dialogue to reinforce the areas of clarity to correct the areas of conflict and ambiguity and decide the decision-making responsibilities for each decision item.

On the sample instrument, I have given my opinion as to how the decision item should be handled. I do not imply, however, that it has to be handled in that manner. The significance of the instrument is that it identifies curriculum decisions that have to be made and gives a method to clarify how the decisions are made and communicated.

Question 4:   Who communicates the decision to all the people who are affected by the decisions?

Studies have revealed that even when the administration is clear about who makes the decisions, this clarity does not filter down to the teachers and to others who are affected by curriculum decision making. This suggests that the problem is not in the decision making itself but in the cummunication of the decision. Therefore, administrators who make decisions in curriculum—especially principals and curriculum leaders—must communicate to the teachers the decision-making responsibilities for all the decision areas. This will reduce the ambiguity that teachers experience in curriculum decision making.

Therefore, every curriculum decision should include a communications component that specifically designates someone to communicate to all affected by the decision who are the primary and secondary decision makers.

The purpose of this chapter is not to promote increased authority for the curriculum leader through increased decision-making responsibility. Instead, the chapter attempts to illustrate the importance of clarity in relation to curriculum decision making and to suggest how this decision-making clarity can be obtained.

Figure 5.1 Decision point analysis

"INSTRUMENT TO CLARIFY DECISION-MAKING RESPONSIBILITY IN A SCHOOL DISTRICT"

Directions: Listed here are several kinds of decisions that have to be made in the process of developing curriculum. Please respond to each decision by placing a check mark or X in the column to the right of the decision item.
You have seven options:

1. Check the first column if you feel that the decision should be made by the *principal alone*.
2. Check the second column if you feel that the decision should be made by the *curriculum leader alone*.
3. Check the third column if you feel that the principal should be the primary decision maker and that the curriculum leader should be the secondary decision maker.
4. Check the fourth column if you feel that the curriculum leader should be the primary decision maker and that the principal should be the secondary decision maker.
5. Check the fifth column, marked *others,* if you feel that someone other than the principal or curriculum leader is the primary decision maker.
6. Check the sixth column, marked *N.A.,* if the decision does not apply in your school district.
7. Check the seventh column, marked *not sure,* if you are not sure what person is primarily responsible for making this decision in your school district.

This instrument is an adaption of an instrument developed by Glenn G. Eye and others at the University of Wisconsin. Additional information with regard to its development is available in *Relationships Between Instructional Change and the Extent to Which School Administrators and Teachers Agree of the Location of Responsibilities for Administrative Decisions* by Glenn G. Eye, James M. Lipham, Russell T. Gregg, Lanore A. Netzer, and Donald C. Francke. U.S.O.E. Cooperative Research Project No. 5–0443 (1913). University of Wisconsin, 1966.

Figure 5.2 Clarifying curriculum decision making

---

1. NAME _____

2. TITLE OF
   POSITION _____

3. SCHOOL
   BUILDING _____

1. Write your name on the line to the left.
2. Write the number of the title of your position:
   1. Teacher
   2. Principal
   3. Curriculum leader (Director of Curriculum, Curriculum Director, Assistant Superintendent, Curriculum Coordinator, Director of Curriculum and Instruction, etc.)
3. Write the name of the school building in which you work.

Figure 5.3 Decision areas.

	PRINCIPAL ALONE	CURRICULUM LEADER ALONE	PRINCIPAL IS PRIMARY; CURRICULUM LEADER IS SECONDARY	CURRICULUM LEADER IS PRIMARY; PRINCIPAL IS SECONDARY	OTHER IS PRIMARY	N.A.	NOT SURE
A. LONG-RANGE PLANNING							
1. Who determines problem areas for curriculum study?				X			
2. Who assigns priorities to problem areas for curriculum study?				X			
3. Who decides the long-range curriculum time line?				X			
B. HOME–SCHOOL COMMUNICATION							
4. Who decides the public relations program for curriculum development?				X			
5. Who decides what news items are to be released?				X			
6. Who approves the content of news items that are released?				X			
7. Who decides who shall interpret curriculum at public meetings?							
8. Who decides on how to gather feedback from the community on curriculum?				X			
9. Who decides on how to report pupil progress to parents?					X		
10. Who determines which community members/parents will be invited to participate in curriculum studies?			X				
C. INNOVATIONS AND/OR PLANNED CHANGE							
11. Who decides if a course of study shall change content?				X			
12. Who approves the content of a new course of study?					X		
13. Who decides the instructional organization?					X		
14. Who decides which teachers are assigned to new instructional/curricular programs?					X		

Figure 5.3 (cont.)

	PRINCIPAL ALONE	CURRICULUM LEADER ALONE	PRINCIPAL IS PRIMARY; CURRICULUM LEADER IS SECONDARY	CURRICULUM LEADER IS PRIMARY; PRINCIPAL IS SECONDARY	OTHER IS PRIMARY	N.A.	NOT SURE
15. Who decides what elective academic experiences will be included in the curriculum in addition to the state requirements?				X			
16. Who approves additions to or deletions from the curricular program?				X			
17. Who decides how to evaluate the success of the teaching of a new curriculum?			X				
18. Who carries out this evaluation process?			X				
19. Who directs the implementation of new curriculum?			X				
D. CURRICULUM EVALUATION							
20. Who decides how to evaluate the ongoing curriculum process (planning, developing, implementing)?							
21. Who carries out this evaluation?				X			
22. Who approves the selection of text books and learning material?				X			
E. IN-SERVICE							
23. Who decides the content of orientation meetings?			X				
24. Who decides what types of activities will be used for in-service sessions?				X			
25. Who decides teacher and staff assignment procedures for in-service activities?				X			
26. Who evaluates the in-service program?				X			
27. Who appoints teachers to curriculum committees?				X			
28. Who decides topics for staff in-service?			X				

Figure 5.3 *(cont.)*

	PRINCIPAL ALONE	CURRICULUM LEADER ALONE	PRINCIPAL IS PRIMARY; CURRICULUM LEADER IS SECONDARY	CURRICULUM LEADER IS PRIMARY; PRINCIPAL IS SECONDARY	OTHER IS PRIMARY	N.A.	NOT SURE
29. Who decides the in-service schedule for the year?				X			
30. Who is responsible for consultants or speakers for in-service programs?				X			
F. INSTRUCTIONAL/STAFF PERSONNEL							
31. Who decides if the instructional methodology is in line with the instructional philosophy?			X				
32. Who decides if the teacher is pursuing the subject-matter content as prescribed by the curriculum guide?			X				
33. Who decides on ways to group pupils?					X		
34. Who evaluates the classroom performance of teachers?			X				
35. Who selects teachers for appointment?					X		
36. Who decides assignments of staff?					X		
G. BUDGETARY							
37. Who determines the amount of money needed for the implementation of a new curriculum?					X		
38. Who determines building budget allocation toward curriculum projects?					X		
H. CURRICULUM COMMITTEES							
39. Who coordinates and directs the work of curriculum committees K–12?				X			
40. Who coordinates and directs the work of building curriculum committees?			X				

Figure 5.3 (cont.)

	PRINCIPAL ALONE	CURRICULUM LEADER ALONE	PRINCIPAL IS PRIMARY; CURRICULUM LEADER IS SECONDARY	CURRICULUM LEADER IS PRIMARY; PRINCIPAL IS SECONDARY	OTHER IS PRIMARY	N.A.	NOT SURE
I. DEPARTMENT HEADS							
41. Who appoints department heads?			X				
42. Who evaluates the performance of department heads?			X				
43. Who decides if the department head is to be retained as department head?			X				
44. Who decides how the administrative evaluation will be communicated to the department head?			X				
J. TEAM LEADERS							
45. Who appoints team leaders?			X				
46. Who evaluates the performance of team leaders?			X				
47. Who decides if the team leader is to be retained as team leader?			X				
48. Who decides how the administrative evaluation will be communicated to the team leader?			X				

chapter six.

CURRICULUM LEADERSHIP STYLES

THE CURRICULUM LEADER'S INTENT and behavior should be directed toward making the role of curriculum leader as tangible as possible. The educational hierarchy is building based: The superintendent is "the boss" of all the buildings. The principal is "the boss" of his or her building. These are tangible functions. All jobs that revolve around the building structure are not as tangible. The curriculum leader should continually strive to make the role tangible in the perceptions of the school and community. Unless the people in the organization clearly know what a person does, that position cannot reach its potential. Clarity leads back to tangible roles. Ambiguity produces intangible roles and, eventually, role conflict. Role conflict and ambiguity have been the major problems for curriculum leaders since the inception of the position.

The curriculum leader should base his or her behavior on the need for a clear and tangible definition and perception of the role. A unique aspect of the curriculum leader role is that it is process expertise based rather than content expertise based. Most educational administration positions are content expertise based: The superintendent is expected to be knowledgeable in school finance, public relations, business management, and so on. The principal is expected to be able to manage the building, administer pupil personnel and staff personnel, and handle like details. A curriculum leader's position is viewed differently. Because of the diverse academic nature of curriculum, the curriculum leader is not expected to be an expert in all content areas. The teachers, supervisors, and other specialists in the content areas will supply the content expertise. What is expected of the curriculum leader is process expertise. The staff expects—and in fact will demand—input into the curricular content. However, the rest of the curriculum development should be planned and facilitated by the curriculum leader. The curriculum leader is expected to be knowledgeable in curriculum planning, design, format, decision making, and evaluation.

These processes are similar regardless of the academic field of the curriculum development. It could be science, math, or any other academic discipline. If the curriculum leader can lead the curriculum development process equally well, regardless of the subject being developed, it can be assumed that he or she has process expertise. Other educators are making the content decisions. However, these content decisions are only a small part of the total curriculum development. Someone must facilitate the whole process. That facilitation of the process, from planning through evaluation, is process expertise.

DECISION-MAKING RELATIONSHIPS

The curriculum leader works with many different groups. Regardless of whether the group consists of parents, teachers, administrators, or students, it is important that the group with whom the curriculum leader works knows its role in the curriculum development process. The curriculum leader should always tell the group what its role is upon initiating the process. Three different roles are possible:

1. *Participants*. The group is an actual participant in the decision-making process. In other words, a decision could be made by the group that the curriculum leader might disagree with. However, the decision would stand.
2. *Consultants*. The group would give input to the curriculum leader prior to the making of the decision. However, the curriculum leader would make the final decision.
3. *Communicators*. The group members are told by the curriculum leader what the decision is so that they can clearly receive and communicate it to those concerned.

All these roles are sometimes appropriate for groups during curriculum development. The key is to make sure that the groups know from the beginning what their role is, and they should also be told why their position is appropriate to that situation.

LEADERSHIP STYLES

Curriculum leadership calls for the use of diverse styles because the curriculum leader relates to diverse groups. The style used should be based on the nature of the question, problem, or circumstances; the nature of the makeup of the group being led; and the time available to accomplish the purpose. Following are descriptions of styles and when they can best be used.

Instructor

The "instructor" style involves the verbal dissemination of information. It should be used when the curriculum leader has knowledge and/or experience that the client group does not have. Therefore, the curriculum leader *instructs* the client groups until they reach a level of knowledge where other styles become more appropriate. This style will be accepted as long as the client group feels that the curriculum leader is capable of instructing it. In fact, it will be welcomed because it prevents the group members from sharing ignorances and will raise their understanding of the topic. Since the style suggests that the curriculum leader has wisdom, the curriculum leader should have the wisdom to know when this style is no longer appropriate.

Troubleshooter

Despite good planning, crises sometimes arise in curriculum development, just as they do in all administrative processes. These usually occur in the implementation process, when monitoring is the leadership mode. The characteristics of curriculum crises involve desperation, lack of adequate time for solution, and/or conflict. However, the troubleshooter style is appropriate only if there is not sufficient time to use other styles. Actually, what the troubleshooter style does is take over a problem that needs immediate attention and maintains a semblance of order until the causes of the problem can be discovered and removed. In the meantime it is hoped that the curriculum leader has, through troubleshooting, stopped the crises from becoming catastrophic.

The curriculum leader will be allowed to troubleshoot if he or she is perceived by the staff as having the commitment, knowledge, and experience to "take over" the problem. Also, the level of desperation must be sufficient that a quick, temporary remedy is necessary. This style should always be a temporary one. But it is an important style. Curriculum leaders who refuse to use it are viewed as weak, "ivory tower" administrators who are only initiators and will not follow through, or who always disappear in times of trouble. Those who properly use the style have taken another step toward making their role more tangible in the eyes of the people of the organization.

Advocate

Any person in a leadership position is expected to have beliefs concerning the area of his or her leadership. Curriculum leaders should have a philosophy of education and theory of administration and curriculum organization and development. Many times curriculum leaders are hired because the school wants their particular curriculum philosophy pursued in the schools. When using the "advocate" style, curriculum leaders are advocating what they think is best for the curriculum. To be successful using this style, curriculum leaders must be confident of their position. The staff must also have confidence in the curriculum leaders. The staff will follow only those advocates who they believe possess expertise. The staff must also be convinced that the advocate fully comprehends his or her own position and has selected that position from many alternatives. In other words, the leader arrived at the leadership position after considerations of many alternatives.

Servitor

In the "servitor" style, the curriculum leader serves the wishes of his or her client system. The leader implements the decisions of the group and facilitates its work by performing the tasks necessary to complete the curriculum development. This style is used in the process stage of curriculum development and is leadership through service. During the curriculum development process many decisions need to be made in which there is no right or wrong. There are many right choices. Therefore, the curriculum leader lets the group make the decisions. This does not mean that the curriculum leader assumes this style only in insignificant situations. There are many significant decisions that can have many correct choices. Another instance in which this style should be used is when the group (teachers, for example) knows more about the topic than the curriculum leader. When this is the case, to use any other style will lessen the quality of the process, whatever phase of curriculum development it may be.

Facilitator

The "facilitator" style differs from the instructor style in that it attempts to bring the group to a level of competence in the total curriculum development concept. The instructor style attempts only to raise the level of understanding in a particular instance, such as one content area. One purpose of this style is to develop curriculum leaders. It requires time and client commitment. It is necessary in organizations that need or desire many people in curriculum leadership. Curriculum leaders may use it with principals. Principals skilled in curriculum leadership may use it with department heads.

A second purpose of this style is to raise the organization's level of awareness and knowledge in curriculum to the point where the people in the organizations will assume advocacy and instructor's styles in curriculum leadership. In other words, the organization would be in an excellent state of health and because of this level of awareness not be in as much need of curriculum leadership. This style is leadership to eliminate the need for leadership. Most certainly, that will never happen. However, what is possible is for this staff to develop a level of ability such that less instruction or advocacy style is necessary. Also, the staff could better serve its own needs and thus rely less on the curriculum leader.

DETERMINERS OF STYLE

As has been previously stated, all the leadership styles are appropriate. The key to good curriculum leadership is to choose the proper leadership style for each situation. The three major determinants of style are time, nature of the question, and the nature of the group with whom the curriculum leader is working. Figure 6.1 is a graph that illustrates the proper leadership style based on the different situations.

HUMAN BEHAVIOR AND CURRICULUM LEADERSHIP

More important to the curriculum leader than all the curriculum knowledge in the world is the ability to know and understand other people's behavior and its implications for curriculum development. The behavior of an individual at a particular moment is usually determined by his or her strongest need. It is important, therefore, for curriculum leaders to have some understanding about the needs that are commonly most important to people.

An interesting framework that helps explain the strength of certain needs was developed by Abraham Maslow.[1] According to Maslow, there is a hierarchy into which

Figure 6.1 Determiners of style.

CURRICULUM LEADERSHIP STYLES	TIME SPAN	NATURE OF THE QUESTION (PROBLEM)	NATURE OF THE GROUP MEMBERS
INSTRUCTOR	Long or Short	1. Solution to question requires knowledge and/or experience that staff does not have.	1. Knowledge and/or experience level below that of curriculum leader. 2. Perceive curriculum leader as capable of instructing them.
TROUBLE-SHOOTER	Short	1. Crises involving desperation, lack of adequate time for solution, or conflict demanding immediate resolution.	1. Perceives problem as being severe enough to require troubleshooter. 2. Perceives curriculum leader as capable of troubleshooting.
ADVOCATE	Long or Short	1. From the political point of view, there is a "right" answer. 2. Curriculum leader's philosophy of education and theory of administration make any other approach unacceptable. 3. Curriculum leader has arrived at his position after consideration of many alternatives.	1. Perceives curriculum leader as person with expertise. 2. Must be convinced advocate fully comprehends his or her own position.
SERVITOR	Long or Short	1. Politically, there is no "right or wrong" answer. 2. Philosophically, there is no "right or wrong" answer. 3. Involves significant question that has many correct choices.	1. Knowledge and/or experience level necessary to make decisions and problem solve. 2. More knowledgeable than curriculum leader on the question.
FACILITATOR	Long	1. Questions involving organizational health such as: • Goal focus • Long-range planning • Communication adequacy (vertical and horizontal) • Resource utilization • Cohesiveness • Morale • Innovativeness • Autonomy • Adaptation • Problem-solving adequacy	1. Possess potential for curriculum leadership. 2. Committed to professional growth and organizational health.

human needs arrange themselves, as illustrated in Figure 6.2. The physiological needs are shown at the top of the hierarchy because they tend to have the highest strength until they are somewhat satisfied. These are the basic human needs to sustain life itself: food, clothing, and shelter. Until these basic needs are satisfied to the degree necessary for the sufficient operation of the body, the majority of a person's activity will probably be at this level, and the other levels will provide him with little motivation.

But what happens to an individual's motivation when these basic needs begin to be fulfilled? Other levels of needs become important, and these motivate and dominate the behavior of the individual. And when these needs are somewhat satisfied, other needs emerge, and so on down the hierarchy.

Once physiological needs become gratified, the security or safety needs become predominant, as illustrated in Figure 6.3. These needs are essentially the need to be free of the fear of physical danger and fear of deprivation of the basic physiological needs. In other words, this is a need for self-preservation. In addition to the here and now, there is a concern for the future. Will an individual be able to maintain his or her property and/or job so that he or she can provide food and shelter tomorrow and the next day? If a person's safety or security is in danger, other things seem unimportant.

Once physiological and security needs are fairly well satisfied, affiliation or acceptance will emerge as dominant in the need structure, as illustrated in Figure 6.4.

Figure 6.2 Maslow's hierarchy of needs.

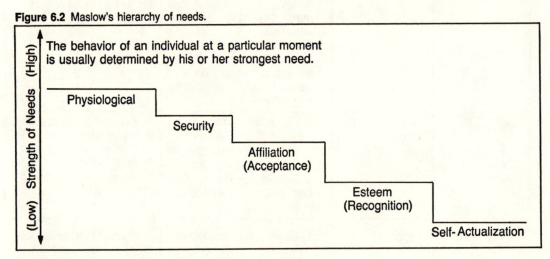

Figure 6.3 Security need when dominant in the need structure.

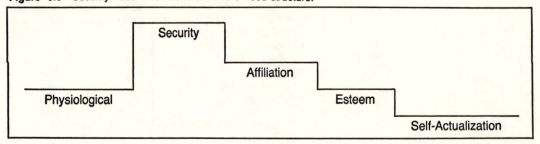

Since humans are social beings, they have a need to belong and to be accepted by various groups. When affiliation needs become dominant, people will strive for meaningful relations with others.

After individuals begin to satisfy this need to belong, they generally want to be more than just members of a group. They then feel the need for esteem, both self-esteem and recognition from others. (See Figure 6.5.) Most people have a need for a high evaluation of themselves that is firmly based in reality-recognition and respect from others.

Satisfaction of these esteem needs produces feelings of self-confidence, prestige, power, and control. People begin to feel that they are useful and are having some effect on their environment. There are other occasions, though, when persons are unable to satisfy their need for esteem through constructive behavior. When this need is dominant, individuals may resort to disruptive behavior to satisfy their desire for attention—for example, a child may throw a temper tantrum or an employee may argue with co-workers or the boss. Thus, recognition is not always obtained through mature or adaptive behavior; it is sometimes garnered by disruptive and irresponsible actions. In fact, some of the social problems we have today may have their roots in the frustration of esteem needs.

Once esteem needs begin to be adequately satisfied, the self-actualization needs become more important. As shown in Figure 6.6, self-actualization is the need to

Figure 6.4 Affiliation need when dominant in the need structure.

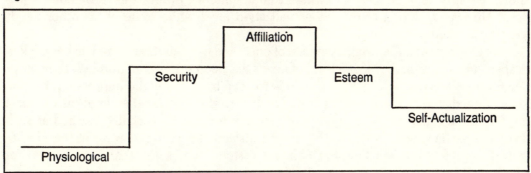

Figure 6.5 Esteem need when dominant in the need structure.

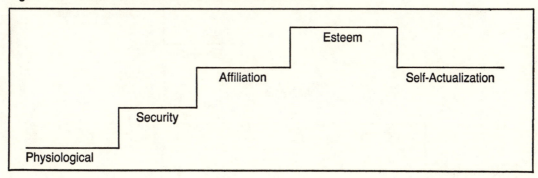

maximize one's potential, whatever it may be: A musician must play music, a poet must write, a general must win battles, a professor must teach. As Maslow expressed it, "What a man can be, he must be." Thus, self-actualization is the desire to become what one is capable of becoming. Individuals satisfy this need in different ways. In one person it may be expressed in the desire to be an ideal mother, in another it may be expressed in managing an organization, in another it may be expressed athletically, and still another may express it by playing the piano.

In combat, a soldier might put his life on the line and rush a machine gun in an attempt to destroy it, knowing full well that his chances for survival are low. He is not doing it for affiliation or recognition, but rather for what he thinks is important. In this case, you might consider the soldier to have self-actualized, to be maximizing the potential of what is important to him.

The way self-actualization is expressed can change over the life cycle. For example, the self-actualized athlete may eventually look for other areas in which to maximize his or her potential as physical attributes change or as horizons broaden. In addition, the hierarchy does not necessarily follow the pattern described by Maslow. It was not Maslow's intent to say that this hierarchy applied universally. He felt this was a typical pattern that operates most of the time. He realizes, however, that there were numerous exceptions to this general tendency. For example, the late Indian leader Mohandas K. Gandhi frequently sacrificed his physiological and safety needs for the satisfaction of other needs when India was striving for independence from Great Britain. In his well-known fasts, Ghandi went weeks without nourishment to protest governmental injustices. He was operating at the self-actualization level while some of his other needs went unsatisfied.

In discussing the preponderance of one need over another, care has been taken to speak in such terms as "if one level of needs has been somewhat gratified, then other needs emerge as dominant." This was done to keep from giving the impression that one level of needs has to be completely satisfied before the next level emerges as the most important. In reality, most people in our society tend to be partially satisfied at each level and partially unsatisfied, with greater satisfaction tending to occur at the physiological and safety levels than at the affiliation, esteem, and self-actualizaton levels. For

Figure 6.6 Self-actualization when dominant in the need structure.

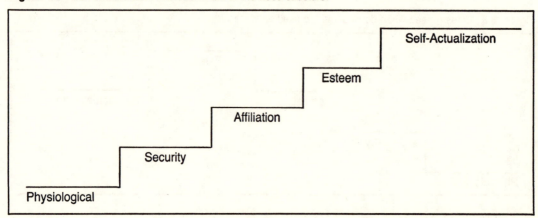

example, a person could be described as 85 percent satisfied in his or her physiological needs, 70 percent in recognition needs, and 10 percent in self-actualization needs. These percentages are used only for illustrative reasons. In reality, they vary tremendously from one individual to another.

MOTIVATIONAL RESEARCH

Having discussed Maslow's hierarchy of needs, we can now examine what researchers say about some of our motives and the incentives that tend to satisfy them.[2]

Physiological Needs

The satisfaction of physiological needs (shelter, food, and clothing) is usually associated in our society with money. It is obvious that most people are not interested in currency as such, but only as a tool to be used to satisfy other motives. Thus, it is what money can buy, not money itself, that satisfies one's physiological needs. To think that money is unimportant at other need levels would be short-sighted, because money can play a role in the satisfaction of needs at every level. Extensive studies of the impact of money have found that money is so complicated an incentive that it is entangled with all kinds of needs besides physiological ones, and its importance is difficult to ascertain. It is clear, however, that the ability of a given amount of money to satisfy seems to diminish as one moves from physiological and safety needs to other needs on the hierarchy. In many cases, money can buy the satisfaction of physiological and safety needs and even belongingness; for example, it provides entry into a desired group such as a country club. But as one becomes concerned about esteem, recognition, and eventually self-actualization, money becomes a less appropriate tool to satisfy these needs and, therefore, less effective. The more individuals become involved with esteem and self-actualization needs, the more they will have to earn their satisfaction directly and, thus, the less important money will be in their attainment.

Implications for Curriculum Leadership. The message concerning money clearly shows why it is important to pay teachers for participating in curriculum development. This payment can come in many forms. There is, of course, direct payment through a supplemental contract or stipend. Or there could be indirect payment, such as paid tuition for college credit.

In addition to meeting the physiological need, paying teachers for curriculum development is saying, "Curriculum development is important." It is important enough for the organization to "put its money where its mouth is." People connect money with commitment and permanence. Both are necessary for successful curriculum development.

A second implication of the physiological needs unrelated to money is the need of food and shelter. Don't misunderstand now—I don't think teachers are starving or freezing. However, most teachers do get hungry after too many hours without food. Most curriculum development meetings take place either in the morning or late afternoon after school. Provide coffee, tea, soft drinks, rolls, and other refreshments for the participants. If the participants are hungry (for food or drink), and whether this hunger or thirst is psychological or physiological, you must meet this need if you expect them to turn their minds to higher thought processes.

The same principle applies to the shelter needs. If the room is too cold or too hot or depressing, comfort will remain the dominant need of the group. Who could write behavioral objectives when their hands were freezing?

If you are asking the question, Are paying the teachers, feeding them, and providing a comfortable environment important to curriculum leadership? the answer is *no*. It is not important; it is *necessary*.

Security

The conscious security needs are quite evident and very common among most people. We all have a desire to remain free from the hazards of accidents, wars, diseases, and economic instability. Therefore, individuals and organizations are interested in providing some assurance that these will be avoided if possible. Gellerman[3] suggests that many organizations tend to overemphasize the security motive by providing elaborate programs of fringe benefits such as retirement plans and health, accident, and life insurance. Although such emphasis on security may make people more docile and predictable, it does not mean that they will be more productive. In fact, if creativity or initiative is necessary in their jobs, an overemphasis on security can thwart desired behavior.

Although concern for security can affect major decisions, such as remaining in or leaving an organization, Gellerman indicates that it is not likely to be an individual's dominant motive. Conscious security needs usually play a background role, often inhibiting or restraining impulses rather than initiating outward behavior. For example, if a particular course of action, such as disregarding a rule or expressing an unpopular position, might endanger one's job, then security considerations motivate a person not to take this course of action. Organizations can influence these security needs either positively—through pension plans, insurance programs, and the like—or negatively, by arousing fears of being fired or laid off, demoted, or passed over for promotion. In both cases, the effect can be to make behavior too cautious and conservative.

Peter F. Drucker[4] suggests that one's attitude toward security is important to consider in choosing a job. He raises some interesting questions: Do you belong in a job calling primarily for faithfulness in the performance of routine work and promising security? Do you find real satisfaction in the precision, order, and system of a clearly laid-out job? Do you prefer the security not only of knowing what your work is today and what it is going to be tomorrow, but also security in your job, in your relationship to the people above, below, and next to you? Or do you belong in a job that offers a challenge to imagination and ingenuity—with the attendant penalty for failure? Are you one of those people who tend to grow impatient with anything that looks like a "routine job"? The answers to these questions are not always easy even though we all understand ourselves to some degree. But the answers depend on how important the security motive is for that particular individual.

Security needs can be conscious or subconscious. A strong subconscious orientation toward security is often developed early in childhood. Gellerman discussed several ways in which it can be implanted. A common way is through identification with security-minded parents who are willing to accept whatever fate comes along. This often occurs in depressed economic areas where the prospects for improvement are poor.

The world seems uncertain and uncontrollable to people raised in a security-minded home. As a result, such people may not feel that they are competent enough to be able to influence their environment.

The security-minded people we have been describing are often very likeable. They are not competitive and therefore do not put others on the defensive. Others tend to expect little of them and thus are seldom critical of their work. This, combined with the fact that these people are pleasant to have around, often enables them to obtain secure, nonthreatening positions in organizations.

Subconscious security motives may also develop in a child through interaction with overprotective parents. Such parents are constantly trying to shield their children from heartache, disappointment, or failure. The supportive attitude of these parents in many instances permits their children to have their own way. Conflict is avoided at all costs. As a result, these children are given a distorted picture of reality and gain little insight into what they can expect of other people and what they will expect of them. In some cases, they become unrealistic in their optimism about life. Even in the face of disaster, when they should feel threatened, they seem to believe that all is well until it is too late.

When these security-minded people leave high school to seek their way in the world, they quickly wake up to reality. Often they find themselves unequipped to handle the hardships of life because they have not been permitted the opportunity to develop the capacity to handle frustration, tension, and anxiety. As a result, even a minor setback may throw them for a loss. Drucker suggests that getting fired from their first job might be the best thing that could happen to such young people. He feels that getting fired from the first job is the least painful and least damaging way to learn how to take a setback and recover from seeming disaster. It makes one better equipped to handle worse fate in late life.

To many people, the security motive carries with it a negative connotation. A strong security need is frowned upon for some reason, as if it were less respectable than other motives. This seems unjust, especially since nearly everyone has some conscious and subconscious security motives. Life is never so simple or clear-cut that one does not maintain some concern for security. In addition, many segments of our society often cater to these needs to the exclusion of such important needs as affiliation and self-actualization. We have already mentioned how industry concentrates on security needs by providing elaborate fringe benefits. Unions have a similar effect with their emphasis on seniority, and the government does much the same thing with welfare and other beneficial programs.

Implications for Curriculum Leadership. The kinds of teachers who are needed for curriculum development are those whose needs are in the affiliation, esteem, and self-actualization domains. Therefore, it is very important for the curriculum leader to meet the security needs of the teachers so that they can pursue affiliation, esteem, and self-actualization. To meet the basic security need of money, work on curriculum projects of any kind should be rewarded by a stipend, honorarium, or supplemental contract. Paying teachers for curriculum work accomplishes objectives other than meeting the security need. It demonstrates to the teacher that the school is making a commitment to curriculum development. It indicates that curriculum development is important enough to be a part of the school budget. If a teacher is making $18,000 per year to teach and is asked to do curriculum development for nothing, that teacher does not perceive curriculum as significant. If curriculum is important to a school, the budget should reflect that emphasis. As has been previously mentioned, security involves more than money. Part of being secure is the feeling that it is all right to be creative or to disagree without fear. The curriculum leader should create an environment that proclaims that disagreement and creativity are acceptable and legitimate, even desirable. If teacher expertise is being relied on for content decision making, teachers must feel secure enough to disagree without fear. Otherwise, the school will have people making curriculum content decisions based on politics rather than on intellect.

The most significant question to the curriculum leader is, *When do people feel secure?* People feel secure when they have been willing to risk their security and have survived that risk. For example, the teacher who has disagreed with the curriculum leader but it still involved in curriculum development has survived a risk and is secure in his or her relationship with the curriculum leader. Encourage risk taking. Survivors of risks become good curriculum workers. In view of the fact that monetary or contractual considerations have been presented in dealing with the security need, it is obvious that the decisions to grant these rewards are not decisions that can be made arbitrarily by the curriculum leader. Therefore the curriculum leader must exert his or her influence with the superintendent and/or board of education to see to it that curriculum development has a sufficient priority.

Affiliation

After the physiological and safety needs have become somewhat satisfied, the affiliation needs may become predominant. Since the human being is a social animal, most people like to interact and be with others in situations where they feel they belong and are accepted. Although this is a common need, it tends to be stronger for some people than others and stronger in certain situations. In other words, even such a commonplace social need as belongingness is, upon examination, quite complex.

In working toward a better understanding of our need to belong, Stanley Schachter[5] of the University of Minnesota has made a significant contribution. His efforts in particular have been directed toward studying the desire to socialize as an end in itself—that is, when people interact simply because they enjoy doing so. In some of these situations, no apparent reward, such as money or protection, was gained from this affiliation.

Schachter found that it is not always simply good fellowship that motivates affiliation. In many instances, people seek affiliation because they want to have their beliefs confirmed. People who have similar beliefs tend to seek out one another, especially if a strongly held belief has been questioned. In this case, people tend to assemble and try to reach some common understanding about what happened and what they should believe (even if it is the same as what they believed before). In this instance, the need for affiliation is prompted by a desire to make one's life seem a little more under control. When one is alone, the world seems "out of whack," but if one can find an environment in which others hold the same beliefs, it somehow makes order out of chaos. This attitude hints at some of the problems inherent in any change.

In pursuing this question further, it was found that when people are excited, confused, or unhappy, they don't seek out just anyone; they tend to want to be with others "in the same boat." Misery doesn't just love company; it loves other miserable people. These conclusions suggest that the strong informal work groups that Elton Mayo found developing in the factory system might have been a reaction to the boredom, insignificance, and lack of competence that the workers felt. As a result, workers congregated because of mutual feelings of being beaten by the system.

It has become apparent by observing "loners" and "ratebusters" in similar factory situations that there is not some universal need for affiliation as an end in itself. It was found, however, that these exceptions to the affiliation tendency were special types of people. They tended not to join informal work groups because they felt either suspicious or contemptuous of them or secure and competent enough to fend for themselves.

Management is often suspicious of informal groups that develop at work because of the potential power these groups have to lower productivity. Schachter found that such work-restricting groups were sometimes formed as a reaction to the insignificance and impotence that workers tend to feel when they have no control over their working environment. Such environments develop where the work is routine, tedious, and oversimplified. This situation is made worse when, at the same time, the workers are closely supervised and controlled but have no clear channels of communication with management.

In this type of environment, workers who cannot tolerate this lack of control over their environment depend on the informal group for support of unfulfilled needs, such as affiliation or achievement. Work restriction follows not from an inherent dislike of management but as a means to preserve the identification of individuals within the group and the group itself. Ratebusters are viewed with intolerance because they weaken the group and its power with management, and to weaken the group destroys the only dignity, security, and significance workers feel they have.

Lowering productivity is not always the result of informal work groups. In fact, informal groups can be a tremendous asset to management if their intentional organization is understood and put fully to use. The productivity of a work group seems to depend on how the group members see their own goals in relation to the goals of the organization. If the group members see their goals in conflict with the goals of the organization, then productivity will tend to be low. However, if these workers see their own goals as being the same goals of the organization or as a direct result of accomplishing organization goals, then productivity will tend to be high. Work restriction is therefore not a necessary aspect of informal work groups.

Implications for Curriculum Leadership. Curriculum development easily lends itself to the fulfillment of the human need for affiliation. Curriculum development requires that people work together in groups, thus providing the opportunity for socialization and other interactions. In education, it is an activity that can break down the isolation many teachers feel. Curriculum development allows teachers to socialize, interact with peers, and have their own judgments about their academic field confirmed, reinforced, or questioned. All of these activities will help the teachers with their affiliation need.

The human need for affiliation is one of the strong rationales for the intensive use of dialogue in curriculum development. Contrary to the teaching process, which for most teachers is largely an isolated experience, curriculum development is a group activity that requires skill in interaction. Be sure that the teachers have sufficient time during which to socialize during curriculum development. Most of the socialization will center on the subject of the curriculum development, because that is the most apparent thing they have in common. Human development activities will help with the need for affiliation by providing the proper environment for good interaction to occur.

Esteem

The need for esteem or recognition appears in a number of forms. In this section we shall discuss two motives related to esteem—prestige and power.

PRESTIGE

The prestige motive is becoming more evident in our society today, especially as we move more toward a middle-class society. People with a concern for prestige want to "keep up with the Joneses"; in fact, given the choice, they'd like to stay ahead of the Joneses. Vance Packard[6] and David Riesman[7] probably had the greatest impact in exposing prestige motivation. Packard wrote about the status seekers and their motives, and Riesman unveiled "other-directed" individuals who were part of "the lonely crowd."

What exactly is prestige? Gellerman describes it as "a sort of unwritten definition of the kinds of conduct that other people are expected to show in one's presence: the degree of respect or disrespect, formality or informality, reserve or frankness." Prestige seems to have an effect on how comfortably or conveniently one can expect to get along in life.

Prestige is something intangible bestowed upon an individual by society. In fact, at birth children inherit the status of their parents. In some cases, this is enough to carry them through life on a "prestige-covered wave." For example, a Rockefeller or a Ford inherits instant prestige with that family background.

People seek prestige throughout their lives in various ways. Many tend to seek only the material symbols of status; others strive for personal achievement or self-actualization, which might command prestige in itself. Regardless of the way it is expressed, there seems to be a widespread need for people to have their importance clarified and, in fact, set at a level that all feel they deserve. As discussed earlier, people normally want to have a high evaluation of themselves that is firmly based in reality as manifested by the recognition and respect accorded them by others.

The need for prestige is more or less self-limiting. People tend to seek prestige only to a preconceived level. When they feel that they have reached this level, the strength of this need tends to decline, and prestige becomes a matter of maintenance rather than of further advancement. Some people can become satisfied with their level of importance in their company and community. In their own evaluation, they have "arrived." Only the exceptional seek national or international recognition. Prestige motivation therefore often appears in young people who tend not to be satisfied yet with their status in life. Older people tend to have reached a level of prestige that satisfies them or become resigned to the fact that they can do little to improve their status.

POWER

There tend to be two kinds of power: position and personal. Individuals who are able to influence the behavior of others because of their position in the organization have position power. Individuals who derive their influence from their personalities and behavior have personal power. Some people are endowed with both types of power. Still others seem to have no power at all.

Alfred Adler,[8] once a colleague of Freud's, became very interested in this power motive. By power, Adler essentially meant the ability to manipulate or control the activities of others to suit one's own purposes. He found that this ability starts at an early age when babies realize that if they cry, they influence their parents' behavior. Children's position as babies give them considerable power over their parents.

According to Adler, this manipulative ability is inherently pleasurable. For example, children often have a hard time adjusting to the continuing reduction in their position power. In fact, they might spend a significant amount of time as adults trying to recapture the power they had as children. However, Adler did not feel that children seek power for its own sake as often as they do out of necessity. Power, for children, is often a life-and-death matter because they are helpless and need to count on their parents' availability. Parents are children's lifeline. Thus, power acquires an importance in children that they may somehow never lose, even though they later are able to fend for themselves.

After childhood, the power motive again becomes very potent in individuals who feel somehow inadequate in winning the respect and recognition of others. These people go out of their way to seek attention to overcome this weakness, which is often felt but not recognized. In this connection, Adler introduced two interesting and now well-known concepts in his discussion—inferiority complex and compensation.

A person with an inferiority complex has underlying fears of inadequacy that may or may not have some basis in reality. In some cases, individuals compensate for this inferiority complex by exerting extreme efforts to achieve goals or objectives that (they feel) inadequacy would deny. In many cases, extreme efforts seem to be an over-compensation for something not clearly perceived although felt. Once accurately per-ceived, the frame of reference can be realigned with reality and result in more realistic behavior.

Adler found another interesting thing. If children do not encounter too much tension as they mature, their need for power gradually transforms itself into a desire to perfect their social relationships. They want to be able to interact with others without fear or suspicion in an open and trusting atmosphere. Thus, individuals often move from the task aspect of power—wanting to structure and manipulate their environment and the people in it—to a concern for relationships, developing trust and respect for others. This transformation is often delayed in individuals who have had tension-filled childhoods and have not learned to trust. In these cases, the power motive not only persists but often becomes stronger. Thus Adler, like Freud, felt that the personality of an individual is developed early in life and is often a result of the kinds of experiences the child had with adults in his or her world.

Prestige: Implications for Curriculum Leadership. It is not difficult to give teachers a feeling of prestige in curriculum development. Their importance can easily be clarified and publicized in such a way to help fulfill this human need.

However, there is one characteristic of prestige that causes problems for the curriculum leader. That problem centers on the fact that young teachers are usually the ones seeking prestige. Older teachers tend to be satisfied with their prestige level or are resigned to their level. Therefore, it is the young teacher who is eager to participate in curriculum development and other improvement activities. The older teachers do not seem as eager to participate. However, it is the older teachers who have the experience necessary for content expertise. The challenge to the curriculum leader is to maintain a self-renewal program so that veteran, knowledgeable teachers maintain a positive atti-tude toward esteem. To take advantage of the young teachers' actively seeking this need, mix them in with veteran teachers for curriculum developments so that their en-thusiasm can be used to the fullest. The combination of the realism of experience and the exuberance of youth is usually a winner.

Power: Implications for Curriculum Leadership. Of the two kinds of power, position and personal, personal power will best serve the curriculum leader. Through-out this book, the claim has been made that the curriculum leadership role is based on expertise, not authority. Let the power of your behavior have the influence. If the cur-riculum leader depends on positional power or legal authority to get things done, that individual's power will be limited. There are too many aspects of curriculum develop-ment where the curriculum leader does not have the organizational or position power. Most likely, it has switched to the superintendent, principal, or teacher. However, if the curriculum leader's power is personal—in other words, derived from the influence of personality and behavior—it will permeate all aspects of curriculum development re-gardless of who has the positional authority.

Another aspect of power that the curriculum leader should pay close attention to is how organizations react to power. Tension-filled organizations have a lot of power seeking, both personal and positional. If there is a lack of respect and recognition among the members of the organization, those who feel inadequate in winning this respect and recognition will engage in attention-seeking activities, many of which are negative and detrimental to the curriculum development process.

Organizations that are not filled with tension will tend to have individuals who seek trust relationships with others. In view of the fact that the success of curriculum development depends mostly on the success of dialogue, these trust relationships will serve the organization well by improving the chances of successful dialogue.

The curriculum leader should strive to create an atmosphere void of fear and suspicion. People should feel free to interact in an open and trusting environment. Thus, the individuals in the organization will move away from power seeking and toward creating trust relationships with others. This is the kind of environment most conducive to good curriculum development.

Self-Actualization

Of all the needs discussed by Maslow, the one that social and behavioral scientists know the least about is self-actualization. Perhaps this is a result of the fact that people satisfy this need in different ways. Thus, self-actualization is a difficult need to pin down and identify.

Although limited research has been done on the concept of self-actualization, extensive research has been done on two motives that I feel are related to it—competence and achievement.

According to Robert W. White,[9] one of the mainsprings of action in a human being is a desire for competence. Competence implies control over environmental factors, both physical and social. People with this motive do not wish to wait passively for things to happen; they want to be able to manipulate their environment and *make* things happen.

The competence motive can be identified in a young child as he or she moves from the early stage of wanting to touch and handle everything in reach to the later stage of wanting not only to touch but also to take things apart and put them back together again. The child begins to learn his or her way around the world of a child and becomes aware of what can and cannot be done—not in terms of what is permitted, but in terms of what is possible. During these early years a child develops a feeling of competence.

This feeling of competence is closely related to the concept of expectancy, discussed earlier. Whether a child's sense of competence is strong or weak depends on successes and failures in the past. If successes overshadow failures, then the feeling of competence will tend to be high. The child will have a positive outlook toward life, seeing almost every new situation as an interesting challenge that can be overcome. If, however, failures carry the day, the child's outlook will be more negative, and expectancy for satisfying various needs may become low. Since expectancy tends to influence motives, people with low feelings of competence will not often be motivated to seek new challenges or take risks. These people would rather let their environment control them than attempt to change.

The sense of competence, although established early in life, is not necessarily permanent. White found that unexpected good or bad fortune may influence one's feelings of competence in a positive or negative way. Thus, the competence motive tends to be cumulative. For example, a person can get off to a bad start and then develop a strong sense of competence because of new successes. There is, however, a point in time when a sense of competence seems to stabilize itself.

Self-Actualization: Implications for Curriculum Leadership. The curriculum leader should keep in mind the following things while working with self-actualized persons: They are more concerned with personal achievement than with the rewards of success. Also, they do not normally seek money for status or economic security. Self-actualized persons want concrete feedback on their efforts. However, they tend to prefer task-relevant feedback, not personal feedback. One caution that the curriculum leader must observe when working with self-actualized people is that many high achievers have a low tolerance for low or nonachievers.

When looking for teachers to participate in curriculum development, the curriculum leader should be happy when some self-actualized people are available and willing to participate. Self-actualized people are usually successful and always ready for a new challenge. The curriculum leader can build on these positive traits. When there are a substantial number of self-actualized people involved in a curriculum development, less direction will be needed. Therefore, the curriculum leader becomes less of a director and more of a facilitator.

Having self-actualized people should be a goal of the organization because self-actualized people are usually the most productive. One of the most powerful traits of self-actualized people is the unusually strong presence of personal needs. Needless to say, they are constantly striving to satisfy these needs. Therefore, the organization should not ask individuals to forsake totally their own personal needs for the needs of the organization. If they do, they cannot contribute to the organization. Therefore, in the context of this book, they cannot contribute to curriculum development. A way must be found to allow the goals of the organization to be met without destroying the personal needs-disposition of the people who make up the organization.

Keep in mind that curriculum development is a social process. The behavior of the participants in curriculum development will be a combination of their personal needs and the expectations of the organization. The workings of this social process and the resulting behavior are well explained in the Getzels–Guba model of organizational behavior.[10]

Getzels' theory is hypothetico-deductive in nature and describes administration as a social process in which behavior is conceived as a function of both the nomethetic and the ideographic dimensions of a social system.

Getzels first presented a set of assumptions and then derived a series of hypotheses from the model. Administration is conceived structurally as the hierarchy of subordinate–superordinate relationships within a social system; and functionally this hierarchy of relationships is the focus for allocating and integrating roles and facilities in order to achieve the goals of the social system. The social system comprises two dimensions: the nomothetic, which consists of institution, role, and expectation; and the ideographic, which consists of the individual, his or her personality, and his or her need-disposition. Two sets of definitions are presented: *Institution* is used to designate agencies established to carry out "institutionalized functions for the social system as a whole," and *roles* are the "dynamic aspects" of the positions, offices, and statuses within an institution. Roles are defined in terms of role expectations, and roles are complementary.

Figure 6.7 shows the nomothetic dimension. Each term on the two axes is the analytic unit for the term preceding.

In the ideographic dimension, for example, *institution* is defined as a set of roles, and *role* as a set of expectations.

It can be seen that a given act is derived simultaneously from both the ideographic and the nomothetic dimensions. The general equation for this relationship is $B = f(R \times P)$, where B is observed behavior, R is an institutional role, and P is the personality of the particular role incumbent.

The proportion of role and personality factors determining behavior will differ according to several variables. Figure 6.8 should clarify the nature of the interaction between role and personality in various situations. It is obvious that, in the military,

Figure 6.7 The Getzels-Guba model.

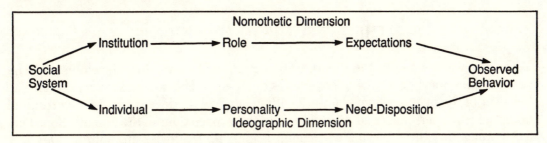

Figure 6.8 Role and personality interaction.

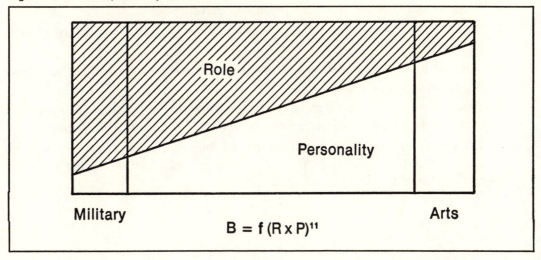

behavior is influenced more by role than personality, whereas in the arts, behavior is influenced more by personality than by role. The proportions should be considered as illustrative and not precise.

Getzels hypothesized that there are three types of conflict to be found in organizations: role–personality conflict, role conflict, and personality conflict.

Role–personality conflicts occur as a function of the discrepancies between the pattern of expectations attached to a given role and the pattern of need-disposition characteristic of the incumbent of the role. Role conflicts occur whenever a role incumbent is required to conform simultaneously to a number of expectations that are mutually exclusive, contradictory, or inconsistent, so that adjustment to one set of requirements makes adjustment to another impossible or at least difficult. Personality conflicts occur as a function of opposing needs and dispositions within the personality of the role incumbent him- or herself. It could be demonstrated (or at least contended) that these hypotheses could be called laws, since they appear to be statements of empirical regularities that now have sufficient proof to be so accepted. In terms of Getzels' theory, these three types of conflict represent incongruence in the nomothetic dimension, in the ideographic dimension, or in the interaction between the two. Within the framework of the theory, it may be generalized that such incongruence is symptomatic of administrative failure and leads to loss in productivity in both the individual and the organization.

THEORY PUT INTO PRACTICE

Let's now attempt to put the theory to the practice of curriculum development. The practice does not appear to be as complex as the theory. The message is very direct: The behavior of the people whom you work with in curriculum development is the result of both their own personal need-disposition and the expectations of the organization. That fact implies that the following curriculum leadership strategies are appropriate:

1. Become aware of the teacher's personal need-disposition.
2. Verbalize this awareness with them so that they *know* you are aware of their feelings.
3. Attempt to meet personal need-disposition if it can be done without upsetting organization expectations.
4. When negative behavior occurs, locate the origin of the problem. The problem can then be defined as institutional or personal and treated accordingly.
5. Do not ask teachers to perform institutional roles that are in direct conflict with their personal need-disposition unless you feel capable of dealing with the conflict that will result.

The dialogue model for curriculum development cries out for self-actualized people because they are the kind of people who will fit the assumptions that are made about the dialogue process. That is, they will be knowledgeable in curriculum content, they can make decisions about scope and sequence, and they can be credible consultants to other teachers.

Following are two graphs that summarize what has been presented in relation to human needs and its implications for leadership.

Figure 6.9 is a description of dominant needs in relation to curriculum development.

Figure 6.10 presents curriculum leadership strategies appropriate to meet dominant needs.

Figure 6.9 Descriptors of dominant need in relation to curriculum development.

PHYSIOLOGICAL	1. Need for additional income 2. Temporary needs according to present environment that come and go quickly: • Hungry • Hot • Surroundings unpleasant • Thirsty • Cold • Sleepy • Need cigarette or other intake • Tired • Uncomfortable • Physically threatened • Need to go to restroom
SECURITY	1. Will not take personal risks. 2. Will not take unpopular positions. 3. Will have conservative and cautious behavior. 4. Does not have capacity to handle frustrating tension and anxiety. 5. Cannot handle setbacks.
AFFILIATION	1. Strong need for personal interaction. 2. Need to belong and be accepted. 3. Uses socialization as an end in itself. 4. Need to have beliefs confirmed. 5. "Misery loves company" syndrome.
ESTEEM	1. Need to "keep up with the Joneses." 2. Desire for prestige. 3. Need to have own importance clarified. 4. Need for prestige is self-limiting. 5. Need for power (personal and/or positional).
SELF-ACTUALIZED	1. This need is satisfied in many different ways. 2. Strong need and desire for competence. 3. Need to manipulate environment and make things happen. 4. Personal achievement is a stronger need than the need for reward or for success. 5. Does not seek money for status or economic security. 6. Strong need for task relevant feedback.

Figure 6.10 Human behavior and curriculum leadership.

DOMINANT NEED OF GROUP OR PERSON	CURRICULUM LEADERSHIP STRATEGIES APPROPRIATE TO MEET DOMINANT NEED(S)
Physiological	1. Pay teachers involved in curriculum development through stipend or college credit or supplement contract. 2. Provide tea, coffee, soft drinks, food, and other refreshments for curriculum workshops. 3. Provide comfortable environment (temperature, seating, etc.) for curriculum workshops 4. Provide attractive environment for curriculum workshops.
Security	1. Legitimize unpopular positions. 2. Create an environment that fosters the feeling that disagreement and creativity are respected, legitimate, and desired in curriculum development. 3. Use in curriculum development teachers who do not always agree with the curriculum leader.
Affiliation	1. Emphasize group efforts in curriculum development. 2. Do not allow isolated efforts in curriculum development. 3. Use dialogue in the curriculum development process. 4. Allow sufficient time for socialization during the curriculum development process. 5. Make human development activities part of the curriculum development process.
Esteem (Prestige, Power)	1. Publicize teachers' efforts in curriculum development. 2. Give curriculum development priority in staff meetings. 3. Maintain a self-renewal program so that veteran teachers will maintain their need for esteem. 4. Keep tension at a low level. This produces trust, which leads to meaningtul human relationships, which improves the chances of good dialogue. 5. Give respect and recognition to staff and other administrators so that they will not engage in attention-seeking activities. 6. Create an atmosphere devoid of fear and suspicion.
Self-Actualization	1. Give less direction and more facilitation. 2. Use intrinsic rather than extrinsic rewards. 3. Assume group competence. 4. Use task-relevant feedback. 5. Do not ask participants to forsake their own needs for the needs of the organization.

NOTES

1. Abraham H. Maslow, *Motivation and Personality* (New York: Harper and Brothers, 1954).

2. Paul Hersey and Kenneth H. Blanchard, *Management of Organizational Behavior* (Englewood Cliffs, N.J.: Prentice-Hall, Inc., 1969), pp. 21–33.

3. Saul W. Gellerman, *Motivation and Productivity* (New York: American Management Association, 1963). See also Gellerman, *Management by Motivation* (New York: American Management Association, 1968).

4. Peter F. Drucker, "How to be an Employee," *Psychology Today*, March 1968, a reprint from *Fortune* magazine.

5. Stanley Schachter, *The Psychology of Affiliation* (Stanford: Stanford University Press, 1959).

6. Vance Packard, *The Status Seekers* (New York: David McKay Company, Inc., 1959).

7. David Riesman, *The Lonely Crowd* (New Haven: Yale University Press, 1950).

8. Alfred Adler, *Social Interest* (London: Faber and Faber, 1938). See also H. L. Ansbacher and R. R. Ansbacher, editors, *The Individual Psychology of Alfred Adler* (New York: Basic Books, Inc., Publishing, 1956).

9. Robert W. White, "Motivation Reconsidered: The Concept of Competence," *Psychological Review*, Vol. 66, No. 5, 1959.

10. Jacob W. Getzels, "Administration as a Social Process," in *Administrative Theory in Education*, Andrew H. Halpin, editor (Chicago: Midwest Administration Center, University of Chicago, 1958), pp. 150–165.

11. *Ibid.*

chapter seven

PLANNED CURRICULUM CHANGE

PLANNED CURRICULUM CHANGE should be based on one of two premises:

1. VERIFICATION OF AN EXISTING DEFICIENCY

Verification of an existing deficiency is a negative premise. However, it is a legitimate reason to alter an existing practice and move toward change designed to correct the deficiency. The verification of the deficiency is a necessary part of this premise. If the deficiency is verified, the support of the change to correct the deficiency will be better.

2. REASONABLE LIKELIHOOD OF IMPROVEMENT

Reasonable likelihood of improvement is a positive premise. It is based on the assumption that even curricula that are not regarded particularly as problem areas could be improved. An organization such as a school should be in a continuous mood of self-improvement. If an organization waits for problems before attempting changes, the number of changes will be small. Also, many change ideas will remain dormant. A very healthy state for individuals as well as organizations is to be in a state of being and becoming—in other words, a state where you feel positive about what you are but you are still trying to be better.

Either of these two premises, one positive and one negative, offers good reasons for planned change to be pursued. Although the motive is different in each case, the process for pursuing planned curriculum change is the same.

TRADITION AND CHANGE
(THE PERPETUAL TUG OF WAR)

If you are a liberal thinker in relation to curriculum, you probably view tradition as the opponent or blocker of planned change. If you are a conservative or reactionary thinker, you probably view tradition as the safeguard against planned change. Regardless of which philosophical position you take, tradition must be dealt with if planned change is the goal. Do not assume that this chapter on planned change is directed only at liberal thinkers. Even the most conservative of curriculum thinkers will at times see the need for planned change and act upon this need. One of the problems in the curriculum change movement in education is that change agents have introduced change without sufficient reason, and conservatives have not changed even when they saw the need. To change or not change should not be decided by the administrative style of people but by the curriculum needs of the school. If the administrators are liberal but planned change is not seen as essential, the schools should have few changes. If the administrators are conservative but changes are needed and verified, planned change should be pursued.

To be successful, the change agent must understand that tradition does not need verification, defining, or defending. However, changes will need extensive verification, defining, and defending. True, this is not fair because many traditions have never been verified in the first place except that for the long period of time they have been practiced. But they have become traditions and, as such, are somewhat sacred to the public and to many educators. Therefore, an attempt to initiate a change that is in direct conflict with a local tradition is doomed to failure. For example, if the use of letter grades such as A, B, C, D, and F is a tradition of the community, a switch to narrative reporting will meet with failure.

Do not conclude from the preceding paragraph that it is impossible to change from letter grades to narrative reporting. However, you may conclude that it is impossible to change from letter grades to narrative reporting if letter grades are the tradition. Once the label of "tradition" has been removed from an educational process, it must defend itself based on fact, data, and other legitimate means. Therefore, it is on even grounds with the planned change. Thus, the change has a chance.

Another example will help clarify the position of tradition in the planned change process. Let us consider a community in which the self-contained classroom is a tradition. Team teaching is then initiated in this community as a planned change. If and when the change to team teaching is attacked, the change will be based on such things as test data and subjective assessment. When the opponents of team teaching begin attacking it, they will know if the students are below the achievement averages, and so on. They may claim also that the students have too many teachers to get to know any of them well enough to feel comfortable. And, of course, they will say that discipline is bad. They will also make the assumption that a return to the self-contained classroom will cure the ills that the change has produced.

In such a situation, the change agent is helpless in defense of the planned change. The change agent is debating against an icon, the tradition of the self-contained classroom. Remember, tradition does not need verification, defining, or defending. If there are any weaknesses in the change in the perception of the community, whether subjective or not, the planned change is lost because a return to the tradition is perceived by the community as an automatic solution.

I hope that the message is becoming clear: Don't plan change against a tradition. Instead, verify that the tradition is no longer worthy of sacred acceptance. Move it to a position where it must be verified, defined, and defended. Thereafter, plan change if necessary or desirable.

COMMON TRADITIONS

One of the first things that the curriculum leader who is interested in or charged with implementing planned change should determine is what the traditions are in the school community. They will vary from community to community. Following is a list of educational practices that are traditions in many communities. It would be wise for the curriculum leader to check the community to see how many of these educational practices are traditions:

1. self-contained classroom
2. 3 R's
3. patriotism
4. traditional discipline values and methods
5. letter grades
6. interscholastic athletics
7. "buck stops here" syndrome for decision making
8. P.T.A.
9. textbooks
10. unquestioned authority of administration
11. subject-matter-centered curriculum-convergent thinking
12. norm-referenced test data
13. Carnegie units
14. traditional attendance procedures (a school day of 8 A.M. until 3 P.M. for all students)
15. competition
16. ability grouping (categorization)
17. teacher-centered learning modes
18. quiet classrooms
19. principal as father figure (paterfamilias)
20. anti-intellectualism (nontheoretical)
21. memory-based learning
22. image of teacher as docile conformist
23. morally based (societal normo)
24. sex stereotyping
25. conformity (dress codes, etc.)

Of course, these are not the only traditions in education. I'm sure there are other traditions in many communities. Make sure that you know all the traditions of your school community. Ways to determine the traditions for your community will be discussed later in this chapter.

Now to the question of traditions that are harmful to students or teachers or schools, or all of them. If it has been verified that a tradition is harmful, the task is to document and publicize the problems. Show the decision makers of the community how the tradition is harmful to the school. Continue this until the community is willing to define, defend, and attempt to verify the value of the tradition. When and if the community becomes willing to do so, alternatives can be presented to correct the deficiencies or improve the process. These alternatives are the planned changes. If the community defines, defends, and verifies the tradition as a valuable process worth keeping, change is not called for. If parts of the tradition are verified as valuable and other parts as problem areas, make changes only in the problem areas. If you as curriculum leader perceive a tradition as harmful but cannot get the community to agree, continue to show how the tradition is harmful. But don't change until the community is prepared to cooperate in breaking the tradition.

The welfare of education could better be served by this process than having curriculum leaders plunge full speed ahead into change that opposes tradition. Spend more time breaking down worthless or suspect traditions. Develop the patience it takes to lay the proper groundwork for change.

The last thing that can be said about tradition is probably the most important. As curriculum leader, work as diligently to preserve traditions that are working as you work to eliminate those that are not. Not only is this the moral and ethical thing to do, but it also adds to your personal credibility by keeping you from being labeled a blind innovator, too liberal, or a change agent who promotes change solely for the sake of change.

COMMUNITY TRADITIONS

The cooperation of certain individuals is needed in order to determine the community traditions. The first group of people required are people who know the particular community very well. They are called conveners. They should have been around the community for a long time and should know people in different parts of the community. Their job is to nominate individuals who represent all the differing value positions or points of view in the community.

The second group of people consists of the individuals nominated who represent the differing value positions or points of view. These people are crucial because their opinions form the data on which the entire investigation is based.

The Conveners' Meeting[1]

The purpose of the conveners' meeting is to identify persons who represent the diverse points of view that exist within the community and to identify the groups of the community that represent these various points of view. The conveners may be school personnel or other persons from the community who are familiar with it. Conveners are chosen because they have a broad knowledge of the various viewpoints that exist within a given community. The number of persons involved in the conveners' process should be from four to seven.

The Meeting Itself[2]

Have on hand a supply of 3 × 5 cards. The following steps are recommended for conducting the meeting:

1. The conveners' meeting will take approximately two hours. There should be a brief, concise welcome and statement of purpose.

2. After welcoming the participants and giving a brief introduction, make the following statement to the conveners: "We are interested in identifying the individuals who represent the various points of view within your community. It is important that you write down the names of individuals who represent all of the differing viewpoints. On the 3 × 5 cards you have in front of you, write one name per card of persons who represent varying points of view within your community." Afterwards, a list of all the names should be made and distributed to the conveners.

3. Next, each convener is given several cards with the following instructions: "You are now asked to write the names—one per card—of the various groups that represent various diverse points of view within your community. The groups may be formal or informal, but it is important that they somehow be seen as a group." Again, compile and distribute a master list. Each group should be numbered consecutively.

4. Now the conveners are given the first set of cards with the individual names on them. For each individual, conveners are then asked to write the numbers of all groups in which this individual is a member. Some persons will be identified as being in more than one group. If another convener has already identified an individual as being in one group and another convener also sees him or her being in that group, they are asked to so indicate by placing the number of that group again for a second time. After a convener has marked all of the cards, he or she then rotates them to the next person until all the conveners have seen all the names. At any time during this process a convener may think of the name of another person or the name of another group, and those names of persons and groups should be added to the list.

5. The conveners are then given a separate card and the following instructions: "Please indicate from the list of groups that you have generated the five groups that most represent the differing points of view in the community. In other words, if you were limited to only five groups and asked to identify the five groups that were most representative of the various points of view in your community, please identify these five groups on this card."

6. Thank participants for their help, inform them when the total process will be completed, and tell them what information, if any, they can expect to receive.

SUMMARY

It is obvious that the data created from the conveners' meeting provide the district administration with a wealth of information beyond that of selecting the participants for the values meeting. It is suggested that the individuals identified go beyond the traditional power base that exists within any community. Indeed, the group should represent all the basic value positions that are evident in a given community.

CONVENERS' MEETING AGENDA
(a quick recap of the convener's meeting that was just presented)

1. Introduction/Purpose: Brief introduction to explain the total effort and specifically the purpose of this meeting. The major purpose is to *identify the various points of view represented in the community*.

2. On the 3 × 5 cards have the conveners respond to the following statement (post the statement on oaktag): "On each card write the name of the individuals you can think of who represent the various points of view in the community. Write only one name per card." *Collect the cards*. Say each name out loud so that duplicates can be put together and a master list can be compiled.

3. On 3 × 5 cards have the conveners respond to the following statement (again, post statement on oaktag): "On each card write the name of the groups—formal and informal—that represent the various points of view in the community. Write one group per card." After the cards are collected write the names of the group on a master list. Number the groups.

4. Redistribute the cards with individual names. Give the following instructions: "On the card naming person A, write the number of the group or groups in which person A is a member." Each convener goes through all the cards. If a person has been already identified as a member of a group and another person sees that person as representative of that group, the convener should list the number on the card again.

5. On another card have the conveners respond to the following: "On this card list the names of *five* groups that are most *representative of the various points of view in the community*."

6. Thank the conveners for their participation.

Selection of individuals to be invited to the values meeting. From the data obtained, the project director selects individuals who will be invited to a values meeting. The group selected should be representative of the range and proportional distribution of the community's values. The degree to which the group is representative of the community is dependent upon the degree to which the persons invited to attend the values meeting are representative of *all* various viewpoints that exist within the community and are representative of the percentage of citizens holding those viewpoints. Clearly, this important step requires knowledge of the community and good judgment. Although this step in the process is necessarily subjective, the value instruments and the nomination of the pool of individuals and groups by the independent conveners, compensate, in my view, for this subjectivity.

The Values Meeting[3]

The following is a step-by-step description of activities necessary to conduct the values meeting. The process as described has worked, is operational, and is open to local revision as may be deemed appropriate.

PREPARATION

1. Using the data generated in the conveners' meeting, select a set of individuals. This set represents all points of view in the community and should be representative of group diversity as well as individual diversity. At least two alternates should be selected for every individual in case the individual selected cannot or will not attend the values meeting. Let the individual who was selected but cannot attend select his or her replacement. The individual will choose someone who represents the same point of view and will probably do a better job of selecting a replacement than you would.

2. A date and place are selected for the values meeting. The place selected should be well known, easily accessible, and comfortable for individuals who represent points of view antagonistic to present school policies and curriculum. Some people are unwilling to attend meetings in what they regard as the "enemy's camp."

3. No more than forty individuals are invited to any one values meeting.

4. A letter of invitation is sent to each selected individual. A self-addressed card is included with the letter. This card indicates a willingness or unwillingness to attend the values meeting.

5. If the card is not returned in five days, a telephone call is made to the individual to determine whether the letter has been received and if the individual plans to attend the values meeting.

6. If an individual does not plan to attend the values meeting, an alternate is selected and the invitational process is started for that new representative.

7. The day before the meeting, all the individuals who have agreed to attend are telephoned by the curriculum leader. The purpose of this telephone call is to remind them of the meeting, to thank them for agreeing to come, and to reestablish the importance of their contribution.

8. Materials needed for the values meeting include:

   a. enough pencils for every participant

   b. masking or adhesive tape

   c. a list of the names and addresses of all people who have indicated their willingness to attend the values meeting

9. Coffee and cookies, or some other kind of snack, should be available and easily accessible in the meeting room.

THE VALUES MEETING ITSELF

1. The person who sent the letter of invitation should attend the meeting and be there in plenty of time to welcome each individual personally.

2. The person who sent the letter of invitation should open the meeting. He or she should thank the individuals for participating, should explain the purpose or purposes of this activity, and should indicate when the data generated by the instrument will be shared with them. If possible, the data should be shared at the end of the meeting.

3. The individual who has invited the participants should then turn the meeting over to a facilitator who will be responsible for explaining and keeping the instrumentation process moving.

4. The values meeting facilitator should emphasize the following points in a very brief introduction:

   a. "You are here to represent yourself, no one else. We want you to respond to the instruments as candidly and as authentically as you possibly can. It is very important that your individual point of view be expressed."

   b. "If you want to receive the instrument you have completed, you must sign your name on the title sheet of the Tradition Identification instrument. For our purposes you are not required to sign your name. So, if you would rather not disclose your name publicly in this way, you are not required to do so. However, we will have no way to return your materials to you unless we know your name. Your name will never be reproduced in any of the materials shared with other people."

   c. "You are going to be asked to express your feelings and opinions about some of the educational practices being used in our schools. We would like you to respond to all the questions asked."

   d. "Your work here today is all individual. We think you will enjoy the activity because it asks you to express your opinion about the educational practices of your schools. The activity is intense, so we hope you will take your time. Feel free to get up and walk around whenever you desire. Coffee and snacks are available and the restrooms are located at _____. If you have any questions, I am here to help—we don't want you to miss this opportunity to express your point of view because my instructions might not be clear. When you have finished completing all of the instruments, please feel free to enjoy our refreshments. After we have taken a break we will share the results of the questionnaire so that you will know what all of you said about each of the questions. Thank you for your participation."

Through analysis of the information, the curriculum leader can determine the traditions of the community. The curriculum leader will then have the basis upon which to proceed with planned change strategy.

Figure 7.1 is the instrument that can be used to gather information about community traditions. Fifteen of the most common educational traditions are used. Other educational traditions could be substituted or added.

Figure 7.1 Tradition identification instrument.

Directions: Following are some educational practices that are used in your local schools. For each educational practice listed, please check the response that best describes your feelings/opinions.

SELF-CONTAINED CLASSROOM

Sample Definition: The practice of having one teacher instruct elementary students in all academic areas (reading, math, etc.).

LIKE/DISLIKE | CHANGE/NO CHANGE

Please check (√) one of the following:

_____ 1. I like the self-contained classroom very much.

_____ 2. I like the self-contained classroom.

_____ 3. I do not have strong feelings, either positive or negative, about the self-contained classroom.

_____ 4. I do not like the self-contained classroom.

_____ 5. I dislike the self-contained classroom very much.

Please check (√) one of the following:

_____ 1. I would actively oppose any attempt to change the self-contained classroom.

_____ 2. I would not like to see the self-contained classroom changed.

_____ 3. I would consider alternatives to the self-contained classroom.

_____ 4. I would like to see the self-contained classroom changed.

_____ 5. I would actively support a change from the self-contained classroom.

LETTER GRADES (A, B, C, D, F)

Sample Definition: Using A's, B's, C's, D's, and F's on report cards, classroom work, and homework.

LIKE/DISLIKE | CHANGE/NO CHANGE

Please check (√) one of the following:

_____ 1. I like letter grades very much.

_____ 2. I like letter grades.

_____ 3. I do not have strong feelings, either positive or negative, about letter grades.

_____ 4. I do not like letter grades.

_____ 5. I dislike letter grades very much.

Please check (√) one of the following:

_____ 1. I would actively oppose any attempt to change letter grades.

_____ 2. I would not like to see letter grades changed.

_____ 3. I would consider alternatives to letter grades.

_____ 4. I would like to see letter grades changed.

_____ 5. I would actively support a change from letter grades.

GROUPING STUDENTS FOR CLASSES
ACCORDING TO ABILITY

Sample Definition: Putting students of the same ability in classrooms together. For example, three groupings are used: above average, average, and below average. Each of these three groups would be in separate classrooms for all academic subjects.

LIKE/DISLIKE	CHANGE/NO CHANGE
Please check (√) one of the following:	Please check (√) one of the following:
_____ 1. I like grouping students for classes according to ability very much.	_____ 1. I would actively oppose any attempt to change grouping students for classes according to ability.
_____ 2. I like grouping students for classes according to ability.	_____ 2. I would not like to see grouping students for classes according to ability changed.
_____ 3. I do not have strong feelings, either positive or negative, about grouping students for classes according to ability.	_____ 3. I would consider alternatives to grouping students for classes according to ability.
_____ 4. I do not like grouping students for classes according to ability.	_____ 4. I would like to see grouping students for classes according to ability changed.
_____ 5. I dislike grouping students for classes according to ability very much.	_____ 5. I would actively support a change from grouping students for classes according to ability.

COMPETITION AMONG STUDENTS

Sample Definition: Students are made aware of how they are doing as compared with other students. Grades are based on the competitive level of the student. Competition against others is emphasized to motivate the student.

LIKE/DISLIKE	CHANGE/NO CHANGE
Please check (√) one of the following:	Please check (√) one of the following:
_____ 1. I like competition among students very much.	_____ 1. I would actively oppose any attempt to change competition among students.
_____ 2. I like competition among students.	_____ 2. I would not like to see competition among students changed.
_____ 3. I do not have strong feelings, either positive or negative, about competition among students.	_____ 3. I would consider alternatives to competition among students.
_____ 4. I do not like competition among students.	_____ 4. I would consider alternatives to competition among students.
_____ 5. I dislike competition among students very much.	_____ 5. I would actively support a change from competition among students.

TEXTBOOKS

Sample Definition: The textbook forms the basis for the curriculum of the class. The content, reading, and discussion that occur in the class are based on the textbooks. All students must use the textbook.

LIKE/DISLIKE	CHANGE/NO CHANGE
Please check (√) one of the following:	Please check (√) one of the following:
_____ 1. I like the textbooks very much.	_____ 1. I would actively oppose any attempt to change the textbooks.
_____ 2. I like the textbooks.	_____ 2. I would not like to see the textbooks changed.
_____ 3. I do not have strong feelings, either positive or negative, about the textbooks.	_____ 3. I would consider alternatives to the textbooks.
_____ 4. I do not like the textbooks.	_____ 4. I would like to see the textbooks changed.
_____ 5. I dislike the textbooks very much.	_____ 5. I would actively support a change from the current textbooks.

THE QUIET CLASSROOM

Sample Definition: The classroom must be quiet in order for learning to take place. Seating arrangements should be made to ensure a quiet atmosphere.

LIKE/DISLIKE	CHANGE/NO CHANGE
Please check (√) one of the following:	Please check (√) one of the following:
_____ 1. I like the quiet classroom very much.	_____ 1. I would actively oppose any attempt to change the quiet classroom.
_____ 2. I like the quiet classroom.	_____ 2. I would not like to see the quiet classroom changed.
_____ 3. I do not have strong feelings, either positive or negative, about the quiet classroom.	_____ 3. I would consider alternatives to the quiet classroom.
_____ 4. I do not like the quiet classroom.	_____ 4. I would like to see the quiet classroom changed.
_____ 5. I dislike the quiet classroom very much.	_____ 5. I would actively support a change from the quiet classroom.

EMPHASIZING THE 3 R'S

Sample Definition: Reading, writing, and arithmetic are more important than creativity and the individual needs of each student.

LIKE/DISLIKE	CHANGE/NO CHANGE
Please check (√) one of the following:	Please check (√) one of the following:
_____ 1. I like the 3 R's very much.	_____ 1. I would actively oppose any attempt to change the 3 R's.
_____ 2. I like the 3 R's.	_____ 2. I would not like to see the 3 R's changed.

_____ 3. I do not have strong feelings, either positive or negative, about the 3 R's.

_____ 4. I do not like the 3 R's.

_____ 5. I dislike the 3 R's very much.

_____ 3. I would consider alternatives to the 3 R's.

_____ 4. I would like to see the 3 R's changed.

_____ 5. I would actively support a change from the 3 R's.

INTERSCHOLASTIC ATHLETICS

Sample Definition: Playing other schools in football, basketball, baseball, track, and other sports with a limited number of students instead of an intermural program involving any students who wished to participate.

LIKE/DISLIKE	CHANGE/NO CHANGE
Please check (√) one of the following:	Please check (√) one of the following:

_____ 1. I like interscholastic athletics very much.

_____ 2. I like interscholastic athletics.

_____ 3. I do not have strong feelings, either positive or negative, about interscholastic athletics.

_____ 4. I do not like interscholastic athletics.

_____ 5. I dislike interscholastic athletics.

_____ 1. I would actively oppose any attempt to change interscholastic athletics.

_____ 2. I would not like to see interscholastic athletics changed.

_____ 3. I would consider alternatives to interscholastic athletics.

_____ 4. I would like to see interscholastic athletics changed.

_____ 5. I would actively support a change from interscholastic athletics.

STANDARDIZED TESTING

Sample Definition: Evaluating how well students are doing by giving them standardized tests that are taken by students nationwide.

LIKE/DISLIKE	CHANGE/NO CHANGE
Please check (√) one of the following:	Please check (√) one of the following:

_____ 1. I like standardized testing very much.

_____ 2. I like standardized testing.

_____ 3. I do not have strong feelings, either positive or negative, about standardized testing.

_____ 4. I do not like standardized testing.

_____ 5. I dislike standardized testing very much.

_____ 1. I would actively oppose any attempt to change standardized testing.

_____ 2. I would not like to see standardized testing changed.

_____ 3. I would consider alternatives to standardized testing.

_____ 4. I would like to see standardized testing changed.

_____ 5. I would actively support a change from standardized testing.

ALL-DAY ATTENDANCE

Sample Definition: All students should be required to stay at the school for the entire school day.

LIKE/DISLIKE	CHANGE/NO CHANGE
Please check (√) one of the following:	Please check (√) one of the following:
_____ 1. I like all-day attendance very much.	_____ 1. I would actively oppose any attempt to change all-day attendance.
_____ 2. I like all-day attendance.	_____ 2. I would not like to see all-day attendance changed.
_____ 3. I do not have strong feelings, either positive or negative, about all-day attendance.	_____ 3. I would consider alternatives to all-day attendance.
_____ 4. I do not like all-day attendance.	_____ 4. I would like to see all-day attendance changed.
_____ 5. I dislike all-day attendance very much.	_____ 5. I would actively support a change from all-day attendance.

SUBJECT-MATTER-CENTERED CURRICULUM

Sample Definition: The acquiring of knowledge (facts, concepts, formulas, etc.) should be the total emphasis of the school curriculum.

LIKE/DISLIKE	CHANGE/NO CHANGE
Please check (√) one of the following:	Please check (√) one of the following:
_____ 1. I like subject-matter-centered curriculum very much.	_____ 1. I would actively oppose any attempt to change subject-matter-centered curriculum.
_____ 2. I like subject-matter-centered curriculum.	_____ 2. I would not like to see subject-matter-centered curriculum changed.
_____ 3. I do not have strong feelings, either positive or negative, about subject-matter-centered curriculum.	_____ 3. I would consider alternatives to subject-matter-centered curriculum.
_____ 4. I do not like subject-matter-centered curriculum.	_____ 4. I would like to see subject-matter-centered curriculum changed.
_____ 5. I dislike subject-matter-centered curriculum.	_____ 5. I would actively support a change from the subject-matter-centered curriculum.

TEACHER-DIRECTED CLASSROOMS

Sample Definition: Most of the time the students should be working as a group with the teacher.

LIKE/DISLIKE	CHANGE/NO CHANGE
Please check (√) one of the following:	Please check (√) one of the following:
_____ 1. I like the teacher-directed classroom very much.	_____ 1. I would actively oppose any attempt to change the teacher-directed classroom.
_____ 2. I like the teacher-directed classroom.	_____ 2. I would not like to see the teacher-directed classroom changed.
_____ 3. I do not have strong feelings, either positive or negative, about the teacher-directed classroom.	_____ 3. I would consider alternatives to the teacher-directed classroom.

_____ 4. I do not like the teacher-directed classroom.

_____ 5. I dislike the teacher-directed classroom very much.

_____ 4. I would like to see the teacher-directed classroom changed.

_____ 5. I would actively support a change from the teacher-directed classroom.

THE TEACHING OF MORALS

Sample Definition: This community has a definite set of morals that the people of the community agree on. Therefore, they should be taught in the schools.

LIKE/DISLIKE	CHANGE/NO CHANGE
Please check (√) one of the following:	Please check (√) one of the following:
_____ 1. I like the teaching of morals very much.	_____ 1. I would actively oppose any attempt to change the teaching of morals.
_____ 2. I like the teaching of morals.	_____ 2. I would not like to see the teaching of morals changed.
_____ 3. I do not have strong feelings, either positive or negative, about the teaching of morals.	_____ 3. I would consider alternatives to the teaching of morals.
_____ 4. I do not like the teaching of morals.	_____ 4. I would like to see the teaching of morals changed.
_____ 5. I dislike the teaching of morals very much.	_____ 5. I would actively support a change from the teaching of morals.

AGE GROUPING

Sample Definition: Children of different ages should not be grouped together. Instead, children of the same age should be grouped together.

LIKE/DISLIKE	CHANGE/NO CHANGE
Please check (√) one of the following:	Please check (√) one of the following:
_____ 1. I like age grouping very much.	_____ 1. I would actively oppose any attempt to change age grouping.
_____ 2. I like age grouping.	_____ 2. I would not like to see age grouping changed.
_____ 3. I do not have strong feelings, either positive or negative, about age grouping.	_____ 3. I would consider alternatives to age grouping.
_____ 4. I do not like age grouping.	_____ 4. I would like to see age grouping changed.
_____ 5. I dislike age grouping very much.	_____ 5. I would actively support a change from age grouping.

P.T.A.

Sample Definition: The P.T.A. is the organization that serves as the liaison between parents and teachers.

LIKE/DISLIKE	CHANGE/NO CHANGE
Please check (√) one of the following:	Please check (√) one of the following:
_____ 1. I like the P.T.A. very much.	_____ 1. I would actively oppose any attempt to change the P.T.A.
_____ 2. I like the P.T.A.	_____ 2. I would not like to see the P.T.A. changed.
_____ 3. I do not have strong feelings, either positive or negative, about the P.T.A.	_____ 3. I would consider alternatives to the P.T.A.
_____ 4. I do not like the P.T.A.	_____ 4. I would like to see the P.T.A. changed.
_____ 5. I dislike the P.T.A. very much.	_____ 5. I would actively support a change from the P.T.A.

RETENTION

Sample Definition: The practice of failing students who do not, in the opinion of their teachers, meet the minimum standards for the class.

LIKE/DISLIKE	CHANGE/NO CHANGE
Please check (√) one of the following:	Please check (√) one of the following:
_____ 1. I like the retention of students very much.	_____ 1. I would actively oppose any attempt to change the retention of students.
_____ 2. I like the retention of students.	_____ 2. I would not like to see the retention of students changed.
_____ 3. I do not have strong feelings, either positive or negative, about the retention of students.	_____ 3. I would consider alternatives to the retention of students.
_____ 4. I do not like the retention of students.	_____ 4. I would like to see the retention of students.
_____ 5. I dislike the retention of students very much.	_____ 5. I would actively support a change from the retention of students.

Interpreting and Analyzing Results of the Tradition-Identification Instrument

UNIQUENESS OF COMMUNITIES

In trying to identify community traditions, you must not assume that educational practices are universally the same. They are not. The name may be the same, but the practice may be different. Therefore, be sure you know what a particular educational practice means in your school community. You should define it briefly on the instrument.

"INTERPRETATION OF RESULTS"

1. Determining the numerical rating of items, by the use of the mean. The rating

is determined by adding the total of the responses and dividing by the number of responses.

Example: Response #1 was 3
            Response #2 was 2
            Response #3 was 5
            Response #4 was <u>3</u>

- Total of responses 13
- Divided by number of responses, which is 4 . . . .
- Average rating 3.25

2. Determining the numerical rating of items by the use of the mode. This rating is determined by the most common response.

Example: Response #1 was 3
            Response #2 was 2
            Response #3 was 5
            Response #4 was 3
            Response #5 was 3
            Response #6 was 1

- The mode is 3

Two different numerical ratings have now been obtained, a mean and a mode. If these two different ratings are identical or similar (± ½ point), the rating should be accorded more validity. If there is a discrepancy between the two ratings, analysis should be applied to find out why. The mode is especially useful in analyzing where specific groups stand in relation to the educational practice.

3. Interpretation of the Rating Scale (use with both mean and mode)

1.0 to 2.5—"Traditional View." Persons or group view the educational practice as a tradition and are thus unwilling to define or defend the practice. They do wish to see it continued. Therefore, to pursue planned change is doomed to failure.

2.6 to 3.5—"More Information Needed." The responses of the persons or group are too noncommittal to be used as a basis for making decisions. More information is needed. Therefore, gather additional information through interviews and discussions before assessing readiness for planned change.

3.6 to 4.5—"Planned Change Possible." Persons or groups have expressed either neutral or negative views about the educational practice. Therefore, planned change is possible. However, planned change should be considered risky because the respondents did not choose the strongest negative response. Also, neutral feelings toward an educational practice should not necessarily be considered as a positive feeling toward planned change.

4.6 to 5.0—"Planned Change Probable." Persons or groups have expressed a strong dislike for the educational practice and have indicated a desire for change. Therefore, it is probable that planned change can succeed.

OTHER IMPORTANT INDICATORS TO BE ANALYZED

Consistency of the Responses: Naturally, the more consistent the responses the more accurate the rating scale. A 3.0 average as a result of three respondents' all checking 3 is a valuable statistic that indicates agreement among all the respondents. On the other hand, a 3.0 average as a result of one 5, one 3, and one 1 response is an indication of disagreement and is thus no value in attempting to assess a community value.

Therefore, the person analyzing the instrument should determine if the rating scale average was the result of convergent or divergent responses. Common sense can be used to answer this question. Rating scale averages resulting from convergent responses should be used in determining community traditions. Rating scale averages resulting from divergent responses should be disregarded.

Group Analysis: The data should be analyzed by groups as well as one total response. This information will be most helpful in attempting to communicate with the community. It will tell you how each group feels about the educational practice in question and, thus, will guide your communication with each group.

If any group averages 1.5 or less, any planned change will probably be severely opposed by this group. An assessment will have to be made as to whether or not to pursue planned change in view of this extremely negative indicator. It could be that the educational practice in question will have to be viewed as a tradition even though the overall rating indicated that planned change was possible or probable. One would have to assess how much influence this group had or if the change was worth the conflict it would produce.

Group power and commitment must be examined in determining the significance of a group's rating scale average. A low rating by one group may be more significant than a low rating by another group. The more politically active the group, the more impact its rating will have on the planned change, either positive or negative.

Contradictions will occur between "like/dislike" and "change/don't change" responses. It is reasonable to assume that persons or groups who indicate that they like an educational practice would not like to see it changed. It is also reasonable to assume that persons or groups who indicate that they do not like an educational practice would like to see it changed. However, that is not always the case. For example, they may not like an educational practice but dislike the alternatives even more. Or they may feel that the problem lies in the way the educational practice is carried out, not in the educational practice itself. Figure 7.2 is provided to help you interpret contradictory responses.

LEADER NOW EQUIPPED FOR CHANGE

The curriculum leader is now equipped with the information necessary to proceed with the change process. The community traditions have been identified. These are not open to the change process. If the curriculum leader feels that these educational practices are harmful to the school and students, a program should be initiated that informs the com-

Figure 7.2 Table for interpreting contradictory responses.

LIKE/DISLIKE COLUMN	CHANGE/DON'T CHANGE COLUMN	IMPLICATION FOR PLANNED CHANGE PROCESS
1	1	Traditional Viewpoint
1	2	Traditional Viewpoint
1	3	More Information Needed
1	4	More Information Needed
1	5	More Information Needed
2	1	Traditional Viewpoint
2	2	Traditional Viewpoint
2	3	Planned Change Possible
2	4	More Information Needed
2	5	More Information Needed
3	1	Traditional Viewpoint
3	2	Planned Change Possible
3	3	Planned Change Possible
3	4	Planned Change Possible
3	5	Planned Change Possible
4	1	More Information Needed
4	2	More Information Needed
4	3	Planned Change Possible
4	4	Planned Change Possible
4	5	Planned Change Probable
5	1	More Information Needed
5	2	More Information Needed
5	3	Planned Change Possible
5	4	Planned Change Probable
5	5	Planned Change Probable

munity about the problems with the practice. It is hoped that this procedure will eventually change the community's opinion and make it willing to define and defend this educational practice. In other words, it will lose its sacred connotation and thus will no longer be a tradition. If and when this occurs, changes can then be considered. If the community's opinion of the educational practice does not change and it remains a tradition, then the change process should not be initiated. The curriculum leader should continue the communication process.

How long one should continue to move the community away from a tradition should be determined by how strong the evidence is that the educational practice is a failure. If the evidence is strong that the tradition is hurting the school, the communication process should continue. Keep in mind that the intent is not to destroy tradition; the intent is to improve educational practices. Communities expect the educators in their schools to be knowledgeable about schooling. Even if the communities don't agree with the professionals, they expect them to have opinions. Even the most conservative of communities expect their educators to present their ideas and recommendations for their consideration. A curriculum leader who continually informs the community of the failures of a tradition is performing his or her professional obligation. No one could ask for more.

The curriculum leader will also know what educational practices the community would consider changing. In these areas, the curriculum leader can proceed with the change process. The remainder of this chapter is devoted to the description of a change model to guide that process.

Bradley Community Curriculum Change Model

The following change model is based on the assumption that it is not pursued in opposition to tradition. It is assumed that the model is being applied to situations that have been defined, defended, and verified to be in need of change through the process described previously in this chapter. Included in the verification process was documentation of the problems that currently exist and are going to be attacked by the planned change model.

STEP 1: VERIFICATION OF EXISTING DEFICIENCY
OR LIKELIHOOD OF IMPROVEMENT

Verification of Existing Deficiency. Verification can be accomplished in many ways. (See Figure 7.3.) If data are available that document the deficiency, the process is considered to be more objective. However, all planned changes do not occur in areas that lend themselves to data collection. Therefore, subjective perception becomes a method of verifying deficiencies. The important aspect of this type of verification is who does the verifying. It is appropriate that four groups agree that the deficiency exists. These four groups are the administration, the board of education, the teaching staff, and the community.

Verification of Likelihood of Improvement. Think once again of the definition of a healthy organization as being one in a state of being and becoming. Even in a healthy organization, there will be room for improvement. In addition, healthy organizations are so successful that what would be considered a deficiency in healthy organizations might go undetected in unhealthy ones. Another category of likelihood of im-

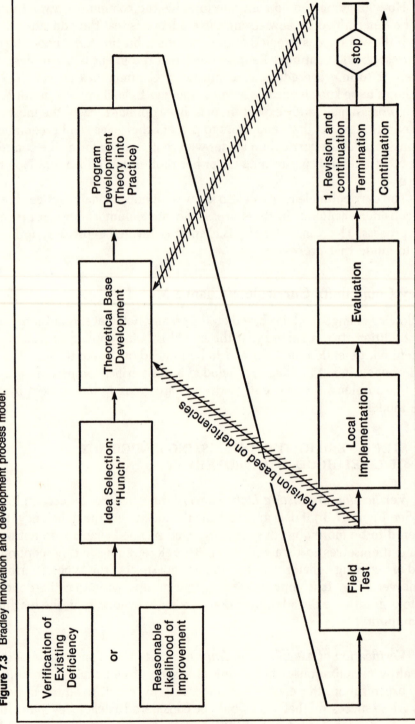

Figure 7.3 Bradley innovation and development process model.

provement would be in an area that may currently be adequate but that is not sufficient to handle future changes.

There are differences between deficiencies and areas that are likely to be improved through planned change. Here are three major ones:

1. A deficiency is producing negative results. Areas of likely improvement are producing satisfactory results (but not achieving potential).
2. Deficiency areas have been defined by all the school populations (community and staff). Areas of likely improvement may not be perceived as such by all the school population. The educators who work with the program daily are most likely to perceive areas of likely improvement.
3. A deficiency is based on local data and assessment. An area of likely improvement may be based on national (outside) research as well as on local assessment. A legitimate reason to change is validated research that clearly shows a likelihood of improvement.

STEP 2: SELECTING INNOVATIVE IDEAS FOR IMPLEMENTATION

Innovative ideas come from many sources, none of which is necessarily better than the others. The most common sources of innovative ideas are:

1. local educators (teachers, administration, etc.)
2. national research efforts by industry, government, private foundations, schools
3. practices (researched and nonresearched) that have been successful in other schools.

Griffiths[4] and others claim that planned change usually occurs from the top down, rarely from the bottom up. This is partly because the administrative hierarchy has no permanent authorized process to hear innovative ideas from its staff. To be successful in planned change, a process must be established and followed to ensure that all local ideas get a hearing. This will keep the ideas flowing.

It is the role of the curriculum leader to encourage and process innovative ideas from the staff. The curriculum leader should also keep abreast of current innovative ideas being researched and implemented in the field of education.

It has been fairly well accepted in education that the curriculum leader is the "idea" person of the school. What has just been discussed is how the ideas should originate.

It is easy to see how the curriculum leader can consider research-based innovation and the innovative practices of other organizations. The marketing techniques of these types of innovation are thorough and easily available to the educator. To solicit and consider local ideas requires some additional organization. First of all, innovative staff ideas should be made legitimate by board policy. Second, the teacher should be allowed to pursue getting the idea heard without undue bureaucratic red tape. If the idea is being considered, the teacher should get the clerical help needed to properly present and pursue the idea.

STEP 3: THEORETICAL BASE

It is the tendency of many practitioners to skip the theoretical base. That is a mistake. Those who do are doing what Van Miller[5] refers to as practice-practice, or, more plainly said, monkey see, monkey do. The theoretical base is the foundation of any practice. It lists for the change agent the assumptions upon which the change is based. This clarifies the change and keeps the later steps of the change process more clearly in focus. For example, if planned change were based around the self-contained classroom, that fact would be a part of the assumptions. Therefore, to deviate from the self-contained classroom is to destroy the theoretical base of the proposed change. If one goes directly into change practices without developing a theoretical base, the assumptions upon which the change was formulated are not clear. Perhaps they are not even written. Thus, they are somewhat indefensible and hard to follow.

You can't get anything done with theory alone. But practice-practice rarely brings improvement, only change. If you are developing your own planned change you must, of course, develop your own theory. If you are adopting a researched-base change you should become knowledgeable in the theoretical base opon which it was developed.

STEP 4: PROGRAM DEVELOPMENT BASED ON THEORY

Program development based on theory is a one-step process in planned change adaption and a two-step process in planned change development. If adaption is the process, this step calls for in-service to the point that everyone involved is knowledgeable enough to implement the program. If development is the process, then two steps are required: (1) develop the planned change based on the theory and (2) provide in-service training for all who will be involved with the implementation.

STEP 5: FIELD TEST

In the adaption process, the results of the field tests should be studied to make sure that the planned change is adaptable to your environment. For example, if the field test results are not as positive in the socio-economic range of most of your students, perhaps it is not the right program for your school. Check the field test results to make sure that the variables upon which it was judged bear close enough resemblance to your environment to safely make predictions for your environment.

In the developmental process, the field test must be done locally. This should be accomplished through project models. These project models should be small in size so that monitoring is easily manageable. In this process, the planned change could be refined and/or revised and sent back to the theoretical base step. If the field test warrants, the change should be terminated.

STEP 6: IMPLEMENTATION

Regardless of the process, whether it be developmental or adaptation, the implementation step seems to be the breakdown point of change. It seems that so much effort goes into the creation and planning of change that the implementation seems to be anticlimactic. It shouldn't be. It should be the aspect that shows the most satisfaction or disappointment. It should be the aspect that has the most monitoring. It was the reason for all the creativity in the first place.

It seems that many change agents lose interest in the implementation process because when the change becomes a reality, it ceases to be a change to them. They turn their attentions to new ideas, step 1. Because of this tendency, change will remain an orphan in education until the emphasis, priority, and interest are maintained throughout the entire planned change process.

STEP 7: EVALUATION

If you believe that the only failure is the failure to try, the evaluation step in the planned change process will hold no fear for you. Change agents fear evaluation only when they have not followed the steps outlined in this chapter and are thus vulnerable and perhaps even overaccountable.

Also, keep in mind that the change should be evaluated against the previous program, be it a then-existing deficiency or an area of likely program improvement, and not against itself.

STEP 8: DECISION MAKING ABOUT THE PLANNED CHANGE

If the planned change is working, continuation should result. Another likely occurrence is that some aspects of the change are working but others are not. However, the pluses outweigh the minuses enough to warrant continuation. In this case, continuation with revision is the proper decision. Make sure, however, that any aspects of the change to be revised are sent back to the theoretical base steps so that the research base can be reestablished.

Termination should be the decision if after evaluation the planned change is perceived as a total failure.

WHY CHANGE FAILS IN THE PUBLIC SCHOOLS

Even in cases where change is not in opposition to tradition, the success rate of change in schools is not good. By looking at Figure 7.4, you can see that change is breaking down at the local implementation and local evaluation stages.

The reason for this is simple. In too many cases, the change being implemented is not the change program that was researched and field tested. Thus the local change is flying on its own with no research base. However, if the local version fails, the evalua-

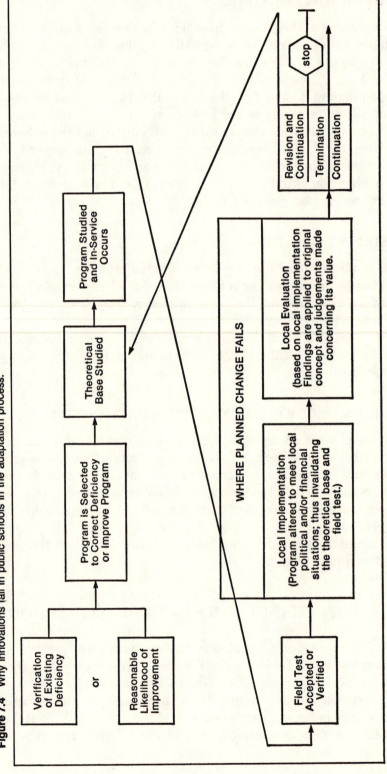

Figure 7.4 Why innovations fail in public schools in the adaptation process.

tion will be presented as though the original change program were a failure. Therefore, the change is branded a failure and terminated when, in fact, what failed was a local version of the change program that had changed the research base and thus invalidated the field test.

Let's illustrate how this destructive process is at work in the schools.

The Individually Guided Education (I.G.E.) Program is a program that has enjoyed much success and some failure in schools. The I.G.E. Program has four major components. They are: (1) multi-unit school organization, (2) league of schools affiliation, (3) I.G.E. learning cycle, and (4) home–school communication.

Let's assume that eleven schools decided that the I.G.E. program would help them. Therefore, a league of eleven schools was formed. Perhaps this component was fulfilled. No more than six of the schools implemented the multi-unit school organization as defined by the I.G.E. program. Only four of the schools implemented the I.G.E. learning cycle. Seven of the schools implemented the home–school communication component.

At the end of five years the league folded. Only two of the eleven schools wished to continue the I.G.E. process. The local evaluations of I.G.E. by the other nine schools found I.G.E. to be failing too many students and recommended abandoning the program. They publicly claimed that I.G.E. had not worked for them. *Something* had not worked for them, but it wasn't I.G.E. It was a local version of some of the ideas of I.G.E. However, it was I.G.E. that was blamed.

As a result of this erroneous assessment, I.G.E. would probably become defunct in the geographical area in which these schools were located. A sound planned change, well researched and field tested, would be terminated in this area, based on an evaluation of some educational practices that were not even close to the I.G.E. process.

Is it any wonder that planned change continues to fail us? We are not giving it a chance. What we should do is stop grabbing bits and pieces from change programs and, thus, implementing with no research base or field test. It would be preferable to carefully select innovative ideas based on verification of existing deficiencies or the reasonable likelihood of improvement and then implement and evaluate without destroying the research base and field test. By doing this, we can begin to sort out which change programs will work and which will not work and, thus, progress.

Under the current state of affairs, we never find out what works and doesn't work, so we continue to swing back and forth like a pendulum. No wonder change is often viewed as a fad that comes and goes and always eventually gives way to tradition. Fewer planned changes will be implemented if the processes outlined in this chapter are followed. However, those that are will be done in a way that will allow for valid evaluation and subsequent continuation, revision, and continuation or termination.

NOTES

1. These techniques and ideas are taken from "The Commission on the Teaching of Morals, Values and Ethics" in the Commission's report to Phi Delta Kappa at Ohio State University, 1980, Suzanne Burkholder, Kevin Ryan, and Virgil Blanke.

2. *Ibid.*

3. *Ibid.*

4. Daniel E. Griffiths, "Administrative Theory and Change in Organization," from *Innovations in Education*, Matthew B. Miles, ed. (New York: Teachers College Press, 1964), pp. 425–436.

5. Van Miller, "The Practical Art of Using Theory," *Organization and Human Behavior*, edited by Carver and Sergiovanni (New York: McGraw Hill, 1969), p. 133.

chapter eight

HOW LEADERSHIP AND DEVELOPMENT COME TOGETHER

BREAKING DOWN A ROLE into functions makes it easier to understand. However, the effectiveness of a role depends on how well it all blends together to make a total performance. Curriculum leaders are not evaluated so much on specific role functions as on how they perform the total role. True, the formal evaluation may reflect specific role functions, but staff and community perceptions will be based on the total role performance. Therefore, it is useful to blend all the role functions together and present a synthesis view of the curriculum leader.

The discussion of the synthesis of the position could be theoretical, but that would not serve to enhance the objectives of this book. A useful way to synthesize the role is to ask two questions: (1) How can it be verified that effective curriculum development is taking place? and (2) How can it be verified that effective curriculum leadership is taking place?

Although these questions are closely related, even sometimes synonymous, it is appropriate to consider them separately. Key indicators can be identified to decide the question of whether or not effective curriculum development or leadership is taking place.

I am not suggesting that these are the only indicators of successful curriculum leadership and development. They are the key indicators from the various role functions, such as task, process, product, decision making, leadership style, and planned change. The indicators will not be separated by role function because this chapter emphasizes synthesizing the job. The attempt will be to blend the roles together and illustrate the key indicators of success. For each indicator, verification evidence will be presented to substantiate its presence.

INDICATORS OF EFFECTIVE CURRICULUM DEVELOPMENT

Because we live in the age of lists, with everything ranked from movies to books and music to sports, Figure 8.1 has been developed to show the top ten indicators of effective curriculum leadership, as well as of development.

Figure 8.1 Synthesis of effective curriculum.

INDICATORS OF EFFECTIVE CURRICULUM DEVELOPMENT	INDICATORS OF EFFECTIVE CURRICULUM LEADERSHIP

<u>Indicator #1:</u> Vertical Curriculum Continuity
 	
Verification Evidence
   -Courses of study characteristics
     -K–12 format
     -No voids
     -No undue repetition
	<u>Indicator #1:</u> Others Seek Out Curriculum Leader for Help
	
	Verification Evidence
	   -Curriculum leader is involved in process and decision making beyond legal authority or formal organizational role

<u>Indicator #2:</u> Horizontal Curriculum Continuity
 	
Verification Evidence
   -Lesson plan content is consistent
	<u>Indicator #2:</u> Curriculum Document Quality Consistent
	
	Verification Evidence
	   -Subject-matter area does not determine quality of curriculum development process or product

<u>Indicator #3:</u> Instruction Based on Curriculum
 	
Verification Evidence
   -Textbooks
   -Learning materials
   -Courses of study
   -Lesson plans
   -Curriculum resource guides are all correlated
	<u>Indicator #3:</u> Teacher Willingness to Work on Curriculum
	
	Verification Evidence
	   -Experienced teachers involved in curriculum work
	   -Repeat participation by teachers
	   -Teachers' verbal feedback is positive

<u>Indicator #4:</u> Curriculum Priority
 	
Verification Evidence
   -Financial commitment by board-administration
   -Philosophical commitment by board-administration
   -Clerical assistance for teachers in curriculum development
   -Meeting agendas
	<u>Indicator #4:</u> Communication
	
	Verification Evidence
	   -Community understanding
	   -Teacher and administrative understanding
	   -Simplicity is accomplished without misrepresentation

<u>Indicator #5:</u> Broad Involvement
 	
Verification Evidence
   -Building representation
   -Principal attendance
   -Quality time for staff input
	<u>Indicator #5:</u> Identifying Working Models
	
	Verification Evidence
	   -Stays within curriculum development time line

<u>Indicator #6:</u> Long-Range Planning
 	
Verification Evidence
   -Written five-year plan
   -Consistent theory-into-practice curriculum permeation
	<u>Indicator #6:</u> Quick Molding of a Workable Group
	
	Verification Evidence
	   -Is able to model proper behavior

Indicator #7: Decision-Making Clarity	Indicator #7: Comprehensive Ownership of Curriculum Development
Verification Evidence -Controversies center on why, not who	Verification Evidence -Teachers feel ownership -Principals feel ownership -Curriculum life span is longer than tenure of curriculum leader
Indicator #8: Positive Human Relationships	Indicator #8: Problem Solving
Verification Evidence -Minimal tension -Positive disagreements -Broad initiation of thought	Verification Evidence -Curriculum leader's willingness to participate in solving implementation problems of principals
Indicator #9: Theory-into-Practice Approach	Indicator #9: Use of Power Over Authority
Verification Evidence -Consistency -Recognizable	Verification Evidence -Curriculum leader's entrusted powers broader than legal authority
Indicator #10: Planned Change	Indicator #10: Use of Multiple Leadership Styles
Verification Evidence -Verified deficiencies data -Reasonable likelihood of improvement data	Verification Evidence -Situations, group type, and time are deciding style of the curriculum leaders

Vertical Curriculum Continuity

The evidence for vertical curriculum continuity can be found in the curriculum documents, especially the graded courses of study. If the continuity is present, the course of study will reflect that curricular voids do not exist. It will also indicate that although reinforcement of learning objectives is occurring through curricular upward spiraling, undue and useless curricular repetition is not present.

Another indicator of good vertical curriculum continuity is the use of a K–12 format for courses of study. This format enables teachers to have quick and constant access to what is being taught in the grade levels below and above them. It is hoped that this also means they are knowledgeable about what is being taught above and below them in the curriculum. And, perhaps most important, the K–12 format provides them with access to enrichment, remedial, or accelerated learning objectives, whichever are needed to meet the individual learning needs.

Horizontal Curriculum Continuity

The horizontal curriculum continuity indicator cannot be verified by using a curriculum document, such as the course of study. Theoretically, if a course of study exists, then curriculum continuity (horizontal) exists. The significant question is, Does it exist in actual practice? The only way to verify the presence of horizontal curriculum continuity is to check lesson plans and observe the instructional process to determine if the intended skills and content are common to all the classrooms of the same grade level or courses that have the same objectives.

Instruction Based on the Curriculum

The quickest verification is that lesson plans are being derived from the courses of study. A second verification is that the curriculum resource guides are being used. Perhaps the most significant verification of all is that all curriculum materials being used are correlated with the course of study. This includes the textbooks as well as other learning material.

Curriculum Priority

Educational priorities are established at the board of education at the administrative level. Board and administrative commitment to curriculum development reveals the level of priority. Basically, the commitment is twofold: philosophical and financial.

The philosophical commitment is revealed through released time for teachers to participate in curriculum development and by providing the clerical assistance necessary to process the curriculum work being performed by the teachers. Providing clerical assistance is a way of saying that the curriculum development products are important enough to take up secretarial and clerical work time. It is also saying that the teachers' expertise in curriculum development is too valuable to waste on typing and clerical duties. Can you imagine superintendents or principals typing their own letters? Important work deserves clerical assistance. Clerical assistance is an indicator of curriculum priority.

Financial commitment to curriculum is shown through payments to teachers for curriculum work. Examples of this are reasonable stipends for work outside school hours and substitute pay for curriculum work done during the school day.

The other important evidence that curriculum priority exists lies in meeting agendas. In school districts where curriculum is a high priority, curriculum topics will appear on board agendas, administrative meeting agendas, and building staff-meeting agendas. These agendas reveal two important indicators of curriculum priority: (1) Curriculum is important at every hierarchical level of the school district and (2) Curriculum is important to personnel at every hierarchical level of the school; that is, the board of education, the superintendent, the principals, and the teachers.

Broad Involvement

A key question is, What is meant by broad involvement? The evidence is very specific and is found in people and process. The people evidence is:

1. Any curriculum development that will affect a school building will have a repre-

sentative from that building during every phase of the curriculum development.

2. Principals attend curriculum meetings that affect their buildings.

The process evidence is:

1. Adequate time is provided for staff input. This responsibility usually lies with the principal. Staff input is best collected at a building level; therefore it is the principal who controls the time needed to gather the input. The principal must provide adequate time not only in relation to quantity, but also in relation to quality. Quality time could be part of the regular staff meeting time. It could be time normally used for instructional planning or other teaching functions. Quality time would not mean that teachers would have to give up their lunch hour, stay after the regular staff meeting, or come in on Saturday morning.

2. Any other group involved with the curriculum development is cognizant of its role. The members can be consultants, observers, or participants. The key question is, Are they sure of why they are there and what role they are to play in the curriculum development?

Long-Range Planning

There are two types of evidence to check long-range planning excellence. One is tangible and the other intangible. First, the tangible evidence: There should be an ongoing five-year plan for curriculum development and/or revision that includes all courses found within the curriculum. Adherence to this plan means that the vehicle for long-range curriculum development is present; that is, that the documentation is present and verified. Now to the intangible evidence: Documents are just paper and ink until people give them meaning. For a long-range plan to be of any value, a philosophy of education and theory of curriculum must permeate the entire school organization. The quality of long-range planning increases in direct proportion to the amount of consistency in this philosophy and theory. A practitioner's way of expressing the "intangible" evidence is summed up in the expression "We know where we are going, what road we want to take, and how we plan to try to load everybody on the trucks."

If the documentation is in place and a consistent approach that permeates the school operation is in process, then long-range planning is in progress. Neither of these can stand alone, for without both, either is fragile.

Decision-Making Clarity

If decision-making clarity is present, the amount of decision-making conflict is, of course, minimal. That is self-explanatory. The significant evidence is that when decision-making controversy does occur, it centers on the nature of the decision, not on who should be making the decision. Controversy over why decisions were or are being made is evidence of a living, committed organization. Controversy over who makes decisions indicates poor curriculum development structure.

Positive Human Relationships

First of all, tension should not automatically be present when the various groups get together. Tension is not hard to recognize. Any normal human being, formally educated or not, can sense its presence. Second, disagreements on curriculum can occur without a breaking down of communication. This means that all are willing to risk disagreeing with anyone else. And last of all, initial thoughts on curriculum come from teachers, principals, and other groups, as well as from the curriculum leader.

To sum up this evidence, good human relationships are present when tension is not. Disagreement is not necessarily a sign of bad human relationships. And initial thoughts on curriculum are coming from everyone, not just the curriculum leader.

Theory-into-Practice Approach

When and if asked, the school personnel, from board to superintendent, to principal to teacher, can tell you what the school is trying to achieve in relation to curriculum. If you examined how the school operates on a day-to-day basis, certain emphases that verify the philosophy of the program would be present on a consistent basis. These indicators could be such things as basic skill emphasis, grading procedures, grouping patterns, promotion policy, homework policy, required curriculum, effective curriculum, general curriculum, specialized curriculum, learning methods emphasized, learning materials, individualization, convergent *vs.* divergent (thinking), or the question of the place of creativity in the curriculum.

The key question is, Are the patterns consistent? It doesn't matter which of these are being emphasized. In the text of this discussion, the important thing is that the practices, whatever they are, are recognizable and consistent. If they are, it is a definite sign of effective curriculum development.

Planned Change

Two pieces of information will indicate the effectiveness of the planned change process. First of all, tangible evidence or data should be on file that planned change is being contemplated or implemented only in curriculum areas that the staff and community will accept. Also, all planned curriculum changes being contemplated or implemented are in curriculum areas that have verified deficiencies or where a reasonable likelihood of improvement has been determined.

INDICATORS OF EFFECTIVE
CURRICULUM LEADERSHIP

Following are the top ten indicators of effective curriculum leadership.

Others Seek Out the Curriculum
Leader for Help

Evidence indicates that given the choice to involve or not involve the curriculum leader in administrative decision making or process dealing with curriculum matters, the principals, teachers, and/or other administrators will choose to involve the curriculum leader. There are many decisions and processes that the curriculum leader is involved in because of his or her position in the formal structure of the organization. However, there are many other decisions and processes that the curriculum leader is not involved in unless other administrators and teachers choose to involve him or her. Also, this formal structure puts the curriculum leader at the mercy of other administrators.

In many instances, the curriculum leader must rely on other administrators for both communication and the implementation of the delivery system. To get to teachers, the curriculum leader must go through the principal. To get to the board of education, the curriculum leader must go through the superintendent. This illustrates that the curriculum leader's involvement in process and decision making is largely in the hands of the rest of the professional school community. They have the option of whether to involve the curriculum leader within some of the formal structure of the school organization. Therefore, curriculum leaders are either broadly involved or narrowly involved in school process and decison making, depending upon how they are perceived by the teachers, principals, and other administrative personnel. The extent of this involvement, determined by others, is a gauge of effective curriculum leadership.

If others are choosing to involve the curriculum leader, that is an indicator of effectiveness. If they are choosing not to do so unless the formal organization gives them no choice, that is a sign of ineffectiveness.

Consistency of Curriculum Document Quality

The essence of effective curriculum leadership is process facilitation, not content knowledge. No one should be able to tell the academic specialty of the curriculum leader by looking at the curriculum products. The process facilitation should be equally effective regardless of the subject of the curriculum development. The effective curriculum leader should have a reputation as a "curriculum person," and no one should be able to ascertain, through observation of the curriculum leader during the curriculum development process, where his or her subject-matter expertise lies. Subject-matter specialists are needed, but the curriculum leader of a school district must be a generalist, knowledgeable and skilled in the curriculum development process. The quality of these processes should not vary significantly because of the content or subject area of the curriculum development.

Teacher Willingness to Work on Curriculum Committees

Another indicator is teachers' willingness to work on curriculum committees. To assess this indicator, check to make sure that experienced teachers are being used in curriculum development—or perhaps, to put it more accurately, that experienced teachers are willing to be used in the curriculum development process. Most inexperienced teachers will participate in curriculum development, but the motive may have more to do with job security than with enthusiasm for the task. Experienced teachers have been around long enough to not feel this particular "need to please." If they are serving on curriculum development committees, then they are doing so for other reasons. It is safe to assume that at least some of those reasons are positive. This is another indication that effective curriculum leadership is taking place.

It is important that the teachers whom the school system considers excellent are participating in the development of the curriculum. Committee representation on curriculum development should contain at least 75 percent representation from teachers who are considered good to excellent by the school system. The other 25 percent should come from teachers with the potential to become excellent teachers.

An informal and interesting way to assess this indicator is to find out what teachers have to say after they have served on a curriculum committee. If they are saying, "What a waste of time," then the curriculum leader has problems. If they seem to indicate that the time and effort were worthwhile, then perhaps effective curriculum leadership is in place.

Perhaps the best assessment of this indicator is how often teachers are willing to serve a second or third time on curriculum development. This is the "proof of the pudding," since they won't come back without a reason. Although serving on such a committee will never rival being president of the teachers' union or head basketball coach, teachers' willingness to serve over and over again indicates that they consider doing so an honor, or at least a privilege. (Considering it a duty will suffice.)

Communication

Communication is an indicator, and it means that the curriculum leader can explain curriculum to the various groups of people who are affected by it. First of all, he or she must be able to explain it to teachers and other educators in terms of classroom implementation. Just as important is the ability to explain the subject to the public in lay terminology. This interpretation must be done without misrepresenting the educational intent.

This ability to communicate with the public on curriculum matters applies to the written as well as the spoken word. Most of the communication with the public is done through school newsletters, flyers, and brochures. The curriculum leader must be able to convey the message without resorting to "educationese."

The curriculum leader must be understandable without being deceptive, or expedient. The curriculum leader's communication skills must include the ability to battle anti-intellectualism. Many people have a tendency to assume this stance in communicating with the schools, and the curriculum leader must be willing and able to accept this challenge.

A curriculum leader should be able to handle this task. If he or she is capable, then communication with the public on the topic of curriculum can have continuity. If the communication is broken up among many people, it tends to become disjointed.

Identifying Working Models

It is vital that curriculum development stay within the time allotted it. A curriculum leader who constantly asks for more time will be thought of as disorganized. Being able to locate the proper working model is the best way to ensure the maximum use of time on a given task.

Quick Molding of a Workable Group

When referring to the quick molding of a workable group, the key word is *quick*. Given lots of time, and by using the proper strategies, it is not very difficult to mold a workable group. If the job must be done more quickly, such as in forty-five minutes, then the task becomes more difficult and calls for a different approach. There isn't time to transfer too much responsibility to the group, so the curriculum leader must count mostly on modeling the proper behavior and hoping that it will "rub off" on the members of the group. Modeling may not hold a group together for two weeks, but it can have a very positive effect on a one-day curriculum development meeting. It is not a replacement for good long-term group-process development. However, it is a good substitute if there isn't time for that long-term development.

Comprehensive Ownership of Curriculum

Too many times in curriculum development the life of the curriculum documents coincides exactly with the tenure of the curriculum leader. This indicates that the ownership of the curriculum never moved from the office of the curriculum leader to the classrooms and principals' offices of the school. If the curriculum leader has been successful in transferring the ownership from himself to the rest of the school community, then he or she has exhibited effective leadership in relation to this indicator.

Although there should be lots of involvement by lots of different people in every phase of curriculum development, it is during the implementation phase that the transfer of ownership must be complete and final.

Also significant in the ownership issue is the question of which teachers show ownership of the curriculum development processes and products. If only those teachers who worked on the curriculum show ownership of the results, that is an indicator that the curriculum leader has not been successful in transferring the ownership.

There are many places where this transfer could have broken down. The most likely place is at the staff input stage. Another likely place is at the in-service stage. Regardless of when it occurs, the curriculum leader must assume the responsibility for the breakdown. Curriculum housed in the office of the curriculum leader is a worthless entity. Curriculum that is a living part of the classroom is a prerequisite for a good school organization. For curriculum to come alive in the classroom, the curriculum leader must be skilled at transferring the ownership from him- or herself to the principals and teachers.

Problem Solving

Even in the best of schools, curriculum problems will occur. When these problems arise, the curriculum leader must be willing and able to participate in the problem-solving process. He or she should be willing to accept that mistakes were made during the planning and/or implementation stage, as well as to participate in attempting to correct them. The curriculum leader must never indicate to a principal that curriculum implementation difficulties are the principal's problem. "Don't call me, I'll call you" should not be the curriculum leader's attitude toward problem solving. Work with the principal in times of trouble. It helps ensure his or her commitment to curriculum.

Use of Power Over Authority

Effective curriculum leaders often work in areas not necessarily within their legal responsibilities. Effective curriculum leaders have many functions entrusted to them that are not vested authority. Therefore, they must perform the function through entrusted power. This power is based on the knowledge, understanding, leadership, or other outstanding traits that make other people look to curriculum leaders for advice and assistance. Curriculum leaders' success in being able to use power instead of authority depends on the ability to gain "entrusted power."

Entrusted power is given because of different circumstances or abilities. One necessary prerequisite is skill in human relations. There are many indicators of effective human relations skills. One is the ability to disagree agreeably. A second evidence is that when disagreements occur, they occur over ideas, concepts, or decisions—not over personalities. A third evidence is that the human relations skills are not built on capitulation. Anyone can appear to be a "good guy" if he or she agrees with everyone just to prevent conflict. But that is not human relations skills. That is weakness, something a curriculum leader can do without.

People tend to entrust power to those who are informed. People also entrust power to those who are willing to stand by and defend their positions. Curriculum leaders who possess these two traits will tend to have power, even in areas where they lack legal authority. If the curriculum leader relies more on power than authority as a mode of operation, a very important assumption can be made: that the curriculum leader is a secure person. Secure people don't need authority. Therefore, entrusted power is much more effective.

Use of Multiple Leadership Styles

The way the curriculum leader behaves while performing his or her role is not always the same; that is, the leader is not always in control, or directing, or trying to persuade, or some other consistently identifiable style.

Instead, the way the curriculum leader behaves while performing the leadership role varies with how much time there is available to lead, the nature of the situation, and the nature of the group being led.

The key evidence would have to be accumulated over time while observing the curriculum leader in many different situations. If the situations, groups, and time span are deciding the style, effective curriculum development could be the results. If the leader's personality is dictating the style, that is not evidence of good curriculum development, no matter how competent the curriculum leader.

Epilogue

At the heart of the current emphasis on educational excellence is a new priority on curriculum development. This priority can only be achieved through effective curriculum leadership which is needed to bring curriculum development to the forefront of education. Theoretically, it has always been there, but in reality, the following parody has been applicable to too many schools.

It is very dark. Through the keyhole shines a small beam of light. The dust is thick, and nothing has moved for fear of being overwhelmed by inertia and resistance to disturbance. The damp musky smell, caused by the lack of light and ventilation, is fed by stagnant moisture seeping in from the adjoining shower room. Only the mice are at home, and even they must look elsewhere for food.

Some things are at home: an ancient water heater, already dead, but still useful to the custodian for spare parts. A vacuum cleaner in storage waiting to be repaired. Some old-fashioned basketball uniforms with leather-like belts and obsolete trim, faded, no longer the right color due to the latest consolidation.

Oh yes, this was the perfect place for these things. Here it was quiet and dead, just like them. The school had passed them by; they weren't needed anymore. They could rest in peace.

But wait: Inside one large cardboard box, something is stirring. Something in there doesn't want to rest in peace. Something feels it and its companions should be alive and in the school.

Suddenly, a key goes into the doorlock. It has to be the custodian, since he's the only one who knows what's in this closet. But he has someone with him: A young person. He's well dressed. A teacher, oh yes, a teacher! At last!

The large cardboard box is radiating with hope. There is a tremendous commotion as all the contents try to climb to the top and be noticed. And read! And used? Such was their hope.

Wham! The box is jolted by a tremendous blow. The custodian is striking the top of the box with one of the old warmup suits to clear away the dust. Coughs are heard, and the air is blurry with dust. Finally, the flaps are yanked away, and the young teacher looks in.

153

"Yes, just the right one on top! Mathematics, my subject!" The book is opened. It is impressive. Outstanding people are acknowledged as the authors. They are respected by their peers. In it, learning objectives are vast, even sequenced. Evaluation techniques are explained, strategies and resources suggested.

The book is ecstatic. It knows the teacher is impressed. Suddenly, its breath is taken. It is falling. Crash! It lands on top of Mr. Music. Dust flies again. More coughs.

As the door closes, and darkness returns, the forlorn math book hears the teacher sigh to the custodian, "Although it looks good, it couldn't be important or in use. If it was, it wouldn't be here."

"Wait!" cries the book. "I am the course of study and the curriculum resource guide! I am the lifeblood of this school! I set the course! I provide help along the way! Without me there can be no evaluation, no coordination or correlation. Without me, you have no goals. Please, oh please, I belong out with the students, teachers, administration. I belong in the classrooms, in the attaché cases. I know you can exist without me, but you can never be whole."

"Oh, what's the use. I'm only stirring up dust for nothing. I'll just lie back down and rest. Maybe they'll come back when they're up for accreditation again. It's only six years away."

The lock is rattled again. This time it's the custodian and the coach. The custodian points to the box and mumbles something about it being just right. The coach enthusiastically agrees, and brags that this will be the greatest homecoming bonfire ever. The custodian also tells him he would like to get rid of the old uniforms, too. The coach vigorously refuses, reminding the custodian that the old-time residents would never stand for the destruction of their colors.

As the bonfire rages and the cheering mounts, one serious mathematics teacher is overheard commenting to a colleague, "Our senior math students are just not ready for calculus. What are we teaching in the other subjects anyway?"

As its last page is devoured by the fire, the math course of study shouts over the cheerleaders' shouts, "Curriculum, instruction, assessment, curriculum, instruction, assessment, curriculum, instruction, assessment. They go together. They go together. But only if you use me. I'm the only way you can know—know—know. . . . "

With your effective curriculum leadership and development, curriculum documents will not gather dust. Nor will curriculum development be an insignificant and peripheral activity for teachers, administrators, and the public. Instead, it will be emphasized. It will become a priority. This is the first step toward achievement of our ultimate mission: excellence in education. What else is there?

Index

Curriculum Decision Making

Presents an evaluation process school districts can use to clarify their decision-making process, which involves all the education community, not just the curriculum leader

Curriculum Leadership Styles

Describes the ''proper'' correlation between the curriculum leader's styles and the particular circumstances, emphasizing knowledge of human behavior and the ability to recognize human needs and how to satisfy them in the curriculum development process

Planned Curriculum Change

Proposes that planned change be pursued only when a verified deficiency exists or a reasonable likelihood of improvement can be shown, and discusses tradition as an opponent of change

Putting Leadership and Development Together

Provides ten specific indicators that can be used to determine if effective curriculum development and leadership are present

WITH DOZENS OF EASY-TO-ADAPT AIDS

In addition, you'll find a variety of charts, forms, and worksheets you can use as they are or adapt to fit the specific needs in your own situation, for example:

- Curriculum Working Model Worksheets that demonstrate how dialogue curriculum is done
- Goal, Objectives, Activity Planning Guides to develop and record a long-range curriculum development process
- a Decision Point Analysis instrument to assess the amount of clarity, ambiguity, and conflict that exists in specific curriculum decisions
- Determiners of Curriculum Leadership Style, a chart to determine which style is appropriate for various situations
- a Tradition Identification instrument to assess the probability of planned change succeeding in a community

For any educator who intends to be a curriculum leader, is a curriculum leader, or hires a curriculum leader, Dr. Bradley's handbook should prove invaluable.